Tortoises

Complete Herp Care

E. J. Pirog

Tortoises

Project Team
Editor: Thomas Mazorlig
Indexer: Elizabeth Walker
Cover Design: Mary Ann Kahn
Interior Design: Angela Stanford

TFH Publications®
President/CEO: Glen S. Axelrod
Executive Vice President: Mark E. Johnson
Publisher: Christopher T. Reggio
Production Manager: Kathy Bontz

TFH Publications, Inc.®
One TFH Plaza
Third and Union Avenues
Neptune City, NJ 07753

Printed and bound in China,

12 13 14 15 16   1 3 5 7 9 8 6 4 2

Library of Congress Cataloging-in-Publication Data
Pirog, E. J. (Edward)
 Tortoises / E.J. Pirog.
     p. cm.
 Includes index.
 ISBN 978-0-7938-2863-0 (alk. paper)
 1. Turtles as pets. 2. Testudinidae. I. Title.
 SF459.T8P573 2012
 639.3'924--dc23

                              2011044443

The Leader In Responsible Animal Care For Over 50 Years!™
www.tfh.com

Table of Contents

Tortoise keeping has been a favorite pastime of people for hundreds of years. In some cultures the tortoise is even seen as a major force of nature carrying the world on its back. In other cultures it is seen as a symbol of long and prosperous life. It is not surprising to see that the interest in the keeping of tortoises in captivity has increased over time. Keeping tortoises as pets can be a rewarding experience, and for many owners the tortoises become more than pets—they become members of the family.

Keeping a pet tortoise (or several) can quickly turn into a larger project. Because of the many aspects involved in keeping tortoises—especially the giant species—the owner might need to learn a little about the engineering, carpentry, veterinary medicine, nutrition, and other fields that may be needed in the quest to provide the best captive care. This learning process usually requires a good deal of work and effort that ultimately proves to be rewarding for both the tortoise and the tortoise keeper. There are many different species of tortoises that are commonly kept in captivity, and there are many basic principles that apply equally to all tortoises with some minor adjustments that are made based on a given species's needs. The main purpose of this book is to provide a general guideline for the

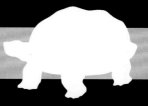

Introduction

basic keeping of tortoises, with some added information for those species that sometimes require unique conditions.

The information in this guide is by no means definitive, because there is not just one way to keep any species of tortoise. View this book as providing suggestions from a veteran tortoise hobbyist to help the new tortoise keeper get started, while offering some unique ideas to the more experienced tortoise keeper. As the new keeper applies some of these ideas it is only natural for the keeper to adapt the methods to fit his or her particular situation.

This guide is a compilation of information obtained from the keeping and studying of over 25 species of tortoises ranging over 35 years of experience. I have kept my tortoises in most of the climatic zones from New York to California, extending south to Georgia in the United States. Further experience was gained through extensive research and correspondence with tortoise keepers throughout the world. Over time I have found that with few exceptions all tortoises have similar basic needs. As long as those basic needs are met the remainder of tortoise keeping becomes much less of a chore and can be quite an enjoyable learning experience in addition to being a pleasurable hobby.

Chelonoidis denticulata

Chapter 1

Choosing and Obtaining a Tortoise

There are many different types of tortoises, so the decision of which one to choose can be quite a daunting task. The keeper must take into account several things, including available space, locale climate, and budget before making any choice of which tortoise species to acquire. Looking at these aspects realistically before actually acquiring the tortoise is one of the most important steps to successfully keeping tortoises.

Space for the Enclosure

The first thing a potential tortoise owner needs to consider is the amount of space the keeper has available for an enclosure. This is largely determined by your living situation, especially the consideration of whether you have a yard big enough for an outdoor enclosure. It would not be very practical for a keeper living in a single-room high rise to consider an Aldabra tortoise—a species that can grow to be almost 4 feet (122 cm) long and weigh 500 pounds (227 kg). On the other hand there are smaller tortoises that would be well suited to apartment living. Several species of smaller tortoises are rare in the pet trade, including the Egyptian tortoise, South African padlopers, and star tortoises. When available these tortoises tend to be delicate and expensive, making them suitable for experienced keepers only. The small Greek and Russian tortoises are better choices for apartment dwellers who are new to tortoise keeping.

When selecting a tortoise, one of the most important considerations is the adult size. Giants, such as the Aldabra tortoise, grow too big for the average hobbyist.

If a tortoise keeper does have the space and the facilities for any of the larger tortoises, some of them make great first tortoises. These species include the African spurred (or sulcata) tortoise, the leopard tortoise, and the Aldabra tortoise. In the case of the Aldabra and the African spurred, it cannot be stressed enough they can get extremely large at an extremely rapid rate. If you can make provisions to accommodate these large and potentially destructive animals, they can be fantastic tortoises to take care of. However, you must think very carefully before obtaining one of these big animals. They might be inexpensive to keep for the first few years while they are still small. As they begin growing and putting on some size, the keeper's wallet is also going to have to increase in size to accommodate the added financial requirement of the tortoise needing a larger and stronger enclosure in addition to the added food intake. It's critical that a keeper thoroughly plan ahead when considering the acquisition of one of the larger tortoises. Never buy one (or any other tortoise) on impulse—no matter how cute they are as hatchlings.

Climate

After considering your space limitations, another factor comes to mind: climate. It is much easier to keep tortoises—especially the big species—if your climate is at least somewhat similar to that of their natural habitat for at least a good part of the year.

Some tortoises come from areas that are humid and warm during most of the year. The tortoises that come from these areas generally do best when provided similar conditions in captivity. This adds to the cost and logistics of providing a suitable environment. These types of tortoises are usually called forest-dwelling tortoises and include the South American yellow-footed tortoise and the red-footed tortoise. These are rather large tortoises requiring warm and humid environments. As long as these aspects are taken into careful consideration, both of these types of tortoises are excellent tortoises to keep.

What Is a Tortoise?

Tortoises are one branch on the family tree of turtles, and the turtles are one of the major groups of reptiles (the other groups being crocodilians, tuataras, and squamates [lizards and snakes]). Scientifically speaking, the turtles are the living members of taxonomic superorder Chelonia. Turtles are sometimes called chelonians, in reference to the scientific name of the group. Chelonians comprise the turtles, tortoises, and sea turtles. Sea turtles are easily distinguished from all the other chelonians in that they have flippers and are found only in the oceans of the world. Tortoises are unique in that they are totally land-dwelling chelonians and all have stubby, elephantine feet. The tortoises are relatively closely related, and all belong to the family Testudinidae. The rest of the chelonians are usually called turtles (and terrapins in some areas), although some may be land-dwelling (such as the box turtles) like the tortoises, and one does have flippers (the Fly River turtle) like the sea turtles. All members of the superorder Chelonia may be referred to as turtles, but only the members of family Testudinidae are properly called tortoises. So remember, all tortoises are turtles, but not all turtles are tortoises.

Some other forest-dwelling species are the Asian brown tortoise and the African forest hinge-backed tortoises (*Kinixys erosa* and *Kinixys homeana*; the other hingebacks are not forest species). The warmth-loving Asian brown tortoise can get quite large and requires either a large indoor enclosure (such as a basement) or an outdoor enclosure, which would restrict its keeping to tropical climates. The African forest hingebacks stay relatively small in size, so providing a humid indoor environment is not that difficult to do. The problem with the forest hingebacks is that captive-born animals are rarely available and wild-caught specimens can be very costly, time consuming, and difficult to acclimate to captivity because of a very high internal parasite load and other stresses related to importation. These tortoises are not recommended for the first-time tortoise keeper.

Good First Tortoises

By far the most commonly recommended tortoises for the first-time tortoise keeper are any of the species of *Testudo*, commonly called Greek or Mediterranean tortoises. These tortoises do not have any overly special requirements and do quite well if provided with just the basic needs of a tortoise in general. With the exception of the marginated and some of the *Testudo graeca* subspecies (e.g., *T. g. ibera*) tortoises, *Testudo* usually stay a manageable size and are quite personable.

Captive-bred Hermann's tortoises—along with most of the Mediterranean tortoises—are excellent choices for first-time keepers.

Another type of *Testudo* that is a popularly kept tortoise is the Russian tortoise. This species has become quite popular and is commonly bred. Russian tortoises are usually available as captive-bred animals, in addition to being farmed. The marginated and *ibera* tortoises can get relatively large, but both also tend to be very slow growers. They are very animated—similar to the red-foots in personality but not requiring the humid environment. Although the marginated tortoise and T. g. ibera are becoming more commonly available in the US, they are still not that easy to acquire. All of these species—especially when available as captive-bred animals—make fine tortoises for the first-time keeper.

Where to Get a Tortoise

Once the keeper has an idea of what kind of tortoise he might like, he now needs to find an outlet for that particular tortoise. The use of the Internet has made this a relatively easy task, providing a good venue for communication with tortoise-specific adoption groups, forums, breeders, shops, and dealers in addition to other tortoise keepers who might occasionally breed their tortoises.

Adopting a Tortoise

Adoption is usually the first choice for obtaining a new tortoise. A word of caution should be noted here. Tortoises can live very long lives, so keepers often make provisions to pass along a tortoise that cannot be properly cared for because of age or other life circumstances the original owner may face. Many chelonian organizations, Internet forums, and reptile specialty publications have classified sections that list tortoises for adoption and sale.

Choose Captive-Bred

Hobbyists are better off purchasing captive-bred tortoises instead of wild-caught ones. Captive-bred animals have a far better chance of being healthy, and they are already adapted to captivity. Wild-caught tortoises often carry parasites and may have suffered from overcrowding, stress, dehydration, and inappropriate temperatures during capture and importation. Additionally, some hobbyists find the capture of wild turtles for the pet trade to be ethically unsound.

Along with specialist groups and online forums, there are reptile rescue and adoption organizations. Most US states will have at least one such agency. Keepers interested in adoption can find them through online searches, reptile magazines, and possibly through local pet stores and veterinary clinics. If you have a local herpetological society, the members are likely to know of any rescue or adoption services in the area. Note that some of these reptile rescues take herps (collective term for all reptiles and amphibians) in general and others are more specialized, perhaps working only with iguanas, tortoises, or pythons and boas.

Sulcatas often are put up for adoption because they are prolific, long lived, and very large turtles.

Hobby Breeders

On occasion private individuals will have incidental tortoise offspring. These offspring are usually sold by word of mouth either on the forums or at regional club meetings. This is most likely the best source for acquisition of a new tortoise, one reason being that it carries the least amount of risk. The purchasing keeper has the opportunity to meet the breeder, who is usually more interested in finding a good home for the offspring tortoises than making a profit. A hatchling obtained from this source is usually well cared for from the start. There is the added benefit of backup support in terms of the proper care for the tortoise, as the person who hatched out the tortoise cared for it and the parents. In most cases the tortoise being purchased is hand delivered, so the person obtaining the tortoise can inspect it immediately, and there is no risk in shipping the tortoise. This gives the tortoise keeper the opportunity to look at the tortoise closely to see whether there are any warning signs of impending problems. It is also a good opportunity to see whether the tortoise will eat right from the start. Many times when a tortoise is moved from its usual environment it will stop feeding for a few days. If the tortoise is observed feeding, that is a good sign it is healthy. Purchasing a tortoise from an individual carries the added benefit that if something does go wrong for whatever reason, the person purchasing the tortoise has a place to turn to for a resolution.

Some hobby breeders are so successful that they have turned tortoise breeding into a small business. These individuals may advertise or rely on word of mouth to attract customers, while quite a few have set up websites showing individual turtles they are selling, and they offer care information. Some breeders have been doing this for many years and have developed good reputations. While tortoise keepers might not get from the large-scale breeder the personal attention they would get from the incidental tortoise breeder—simply due to the number of animals the large-scale breeder produces—the customer service and level of care the tortoises receive are still very good.

You can often find these breeders at the various reptile shows where they display the animals they have available for sale. (Reptile shows are also called herp shows, herp expos, and reptile expos). Buyers at these shows have the opportunity to examine the tortoises they are interested in purchasing. There is also the opportunity to talk to the breeder. Many breeders also offer care sheets and further support after the purchase of the tortoise. It can be a bit riskier to buy from a breeder who does not offer this kind of support, because it may indicate how much time he may be willing to devote to a customer who has a problem.

Pet Shops

Pet shops are usually not a good source for the purchase of a tortoise. For the most part these shops have little experience in dealing with tortoises. With the help of well-intentioned tortoise keepers and organizations, this situation does seem to be changing for the better with the aid of care sheets in addition to open dialog and education with some pet shop keepers. However, pet shops vary greatly in quality. If your local store takes good care of its animals and has experienced reptile keepers on staff, it may be fine place to buy a tortoise.

The tortoises available from hobby breeders are usually very healthy and well-cared for.

Do Tortoises Need Company?

A common question that comes up with first-time tortoise keepers is whether they should keep more than one. Tortoises are solitary animals for the most part, but they do seem to benefit from the interaction of more than one animal. However, when keeping tortoises of the same sex—whether two males or two females—this interaction is not always a positive one. Negative interactions can also occur between a male and a female. While negative interaction between male and female tortoises kept together is not a very common occurrence, it can lead to one or more of the tortoises getting physically injured. In most cases injuries usually do not occur if the turtles are given enough space and the enclosure has proper furnishings. If this becomes a concern the tortoises can easily be kept in a solitary situation without any problems. Don't be concerned about keeping just one tortoise or keeping each tortoise in its own enclosure. Tortoises most likely do not experience loneliness, and tortoises kept by themselves do just fine.

There are specialty pet shops that focus on amphibians and reptiles. Many of these pet shops are very good sources for obtaining a tortoise. The tortoises may not be getting the same level of care as those offered by hobby breeders, but most of the time the staff will be providing appropriate housing and diet for the species. The tortoises in these shops usually do not spend a great deal of time in the shop, because they are purchased and replaced. A specialty shop's tortoises may come from a multitude of sources, so the health risks are increased, but the more reputable shops will offer some form of guarantee. These shops may offer captive-bred tortoises. There are many incidental tortoise breeders who would rather not deal with the general public. They end up selling their offspring to shops all at once so they do not have to deal with individual sales or housing the hatchlings for a long time. Some specialty pet shops also breed some of their own animals.

If you are considering purchasing your tortoise at a pet store (or other source you can actually visit) it is a good idea to look over the facilities. Pay attention to see whether the water bowls are clean and filled. Check to see how the animals are cared for in terms of generally clean enclosures and substrate. Keep in mind that pet stores are just holding areas before the animal finds a permanent home, and therefore don't expect the care to be perfect. For example, the enclosures are likely to be too small for long-term care. What the keeper should be looking for is whether the basic needs of the animal are being met and the animal looks healthy and clean. Temperature and diet should be appropriate for the species. Then ask around on the forums and the local organizations to see whether anyone has dealt with that particular shop. If the shop has had some bad dealings, word will get around. When a shop develops a good reputation, the word will get around also.

Tortoise Farms

A relatively new trend in the herp hobby is the establishment of breeding farms. These are facilities where wild-caught tortoises are set up in large pens similar to the way cattle are raised. These farms are usually set up in a country where the tortoises naturally occur or in a place with a climate that is very similar to the place of origin of the tortoises. Normally the farmed tortoises are very well cared for. The tortoises go on to eventually breed and lay eggs. The eggs are collected and incubated until they hatch. The offspring are usually raised to a suitable size and shipped off to various shops and dealers.

This has successfully been accomplished with many tortoises, including red-footed tortoises, leopard tortoises, Russian tortoises, marginated tortoises, and Hermann's tortoises, among others. Because of the crowded conditions these tortoises are often kept in, it is a good idea to have them checked by a veterinarian. They should be treated prophylactically for protozoans regardless, just to be on the safe side. This will dramatically decrease the chances of any problems developing. The advantage of obtaining

A healthy tortoise has clear eyes, has no discharge from the nostrils, and is alert and interested in its surroundings.

these tortoises is that they are head-started beyond the first year, which is the most delicate stage in the development of a tortoise. Farm-raised tortoises are usually less expensive than equal-size tortoises from any other source. Farm-raised tortoises are more available in Europe than in the United States, but they are becoming more common in American pet stores and reptile shows.

Online Vendors

The last source for a keeper to consider is online or Internet tortoise distributors. These are not the same as breeders who are selling online; they are larger facilities that often deal in many different animals and possibly in selling supplies and equipment. The keeper needs to be very careful when dealing with online sources. It is very easy to get taken advantage of on the Internet because you are dealing with a person who is sight unseen and there is little recourse once you send your money. Most Internet outlets for tortoises will only ship the tortoise—you won't be able to pick it up. It is highly risky to deal with shipping a tortoise throughout much of the year unless extreme care is exercised in the preparation and the packing of the shipment. Sometimes the dealer and the buyer can arrange to meet at one of the local reptile shows. This is always a good idea, because the keeper making the purchase can actually see the desired tortoise, meet the seller, and avoid the expense and risk of shipping. There are reputable dealers, but keepers need to do a great deal of research to be relatively sure they are getting what they pay for. A keeper should ask on the forums about

Warning Signs

There are certain important things you should watch out for when you are trying to pick out a healthy tortoise. If the tortoise you are considering displays one or more of the following signs, it would be best to avoid that particular animal:

- Caked feces or discharge around the vent or back end of the shell
- Feeling light in weight for its size
- Limbs not functioning properly
- Listlessness or inactivity
- Loose, watery, or bloody feces
- Soft shell
- Sunken or closed eyes
- Watery eyes or runny nose

The size difference between hatchling and adult tortoises can be enormous. Before bringing home a cute little hatchling, plan for the adult size.

other keepers' dealings with any individual. Many websites have a review section or are reviewed on various forums.

Selecting a Healthy Tortoise

The keeper should always try to physically see a new tortoise before obtaining it. If dealing with a source on the Internet, it is always a good idea to ask for as many photos of the tortoise as possible to properly evaluate the turtle.

The key physical health indicators the keeper should look for are that the tortoise should be active, with no discharge coming from the nose. The tortoise might not want to cooperate in terms of being active, but this is an important point and the tortoise should be encouraged to move about. This can be accomplished by coaxing the tortoise with food or placing the tortoise in a shallow pool of water. Ask the seller to help in getting the tortoise active if it is not active already. Experienced keepers usually know how to get a tortoise moving. If it is not very active it is not a good idea to purchase that particular tortoise.

Any tortoise with a nasal discharge, such as a watery discharge or a thicker mucus discharge, should be avoided. The nasal openings should be clear and dry. The eyes should be fully open, round, and bright. Look for any indication of the eyes being sunken in, which is a sign of ill health and possible dehydration. It is an added assurance if the keeper can witness the tortoise eating. The tortoise should have a good muscular look to the front and back legs, without a sunken look to the head, neck, or legs. The sunken look can be a sign of ill health, dehydration, or malnutrition.

Preparing for the Tortoise

The basic process of how to choose a tortoise is not an easy one. The keeper can always change his mind as he learns more about tortoises. The situation is going to change as the keeper then prepares the accommodations and supplies for the tortoise. The final decision is going to be based on what the keeper can actually provide with what is available to him.

It is always best to have the enclosure set up before actually bringing home the tortoise. This prevents having the tortoise sit in a box while the keeper scrambles to assemble the necessary items. The keeper needs to have an enclosure of the proper size ready for the animal. By setting it up beforehand, the keeper can be sure that the temperatures and humidity are appropriate for a given species.

When many pet owners decide to add a pet to the household, they do not give much consideration to what they are going to do if the pet becomes ill or injured. If all goes well in the selection and the acquisition of the tortoise this should not be a concern right at the beginning— but it's best to make provisions for these misfortunes before they actually happen. This is why the keeper should find a good reptile veterinarian before it is actually necessary. For suggestions on finding a reptile veterinarian, refer to Chapter 5: Health Care.

Mixing Species

Many new keepers would like to have more than one tortoise. Some of those keepers would like to get two different tortoises, which brings up the topic of mixing species. In the past this was a bad idea and still is with wild-caught tortoises because most of them are heavily infested with parasites and possibly viruses to which other species might be especially vulnerable. Most tortoises that are available today are captive born and raised. If the tortoises in question have the same environmental requirements there should be no reason they cannot be kept together. There may be some concern about hybridization, but this rarely occurs.

Tortoise Anatomy

vertebrals

nuchal

costals

marginals

costals

eye

beak

carpace

plastron

marginals

claws

carapace: top part of the shell
plastron: bottom part of the shell
SCL: abbreviation for Straight Carapace Length
scute: the individual plates that make up the shell

The scutes are named according to their position:
costal scutes: scutes on the side of the carapace between the marginals and the vertebrals

marginal scute: scutes on the outer edge of the carapace
nuchal scute: scute directly above the neck (absent in some species)
vertebral scute: scutes on the midline of the carapace; the scutes directly above the spinal column

Testudo horsfieldi

Chapter 2

Housing

Housing is probably the most important aspect of tortoise keeping because it deals with the two most important needs for the proper development of a tortoise: heat and hydration. These two critical points are going to be stressed throughout this guide. Without careful attention to these two basic components, the rest of the tortoise's biological processes cannot take place. Housing also provides the environment the tortoise requires to feel comfortable enough to behave naturally.

Outdoor housing is always best for tortoises because it gives them access to natural sunlight and more space than indoor housing.

After selecting the species you want, the most important consideration is providing good accommodations for that tortoise. How you house your tortoise will depend mostly on the species and whether you are planning to obtain a hatchling, full-grown adult, or something in between. There are two major methods of housing tortoises: indoors and outdoors. The climate the keeper lives in will determine whether outdoor housing is possible for at least some part of the year. If the keeper is fortunate enough to live in a climate where the tortoise can be kept outdoors all year round, this is the most ideal situation for the tortoise and the keeper. It is always healthier for the tortoise and easier for the keeper to maintain tortoises outdoors. Unfortunately, that is not possible for many keepers. As you move away from the Equator to the more northern or southern latitudes, it becomes more difficult to maintain tortoises outdoors to the point that it is not possible to keep a tortoise outdoors at all if you go very far. If the keeper does decide to try and keep any of the larger tortoises, such as the African spurred or Aldabra tortoises, in such cooler climates, it becomes a very difficult and costly project. In the warmer climates keeping a really large species is much more practical and realistic.

Indoor Housing

There are many choices for providing indoor housing, and if the keeper is a good craftsman who can build accommodations, the possibilities expand. When considering the basic enclosure, the tortoise keeper should provide as much space for the tortoise as possible. The enclosure should be high enough for the tortoise not to be able to climb out. The enclosure should also have enough floor space to provide adequate room for the tortoise to move about freely. A general guideline to the basic dimensions would be to provide a height of three times the length of the tortoise with a width of five times the length of the tortoise and a length of ten times the length of the tortoise; consider this the minimum size for an enclosure. So a tortoise that is a foot (30.5 cm) long would need an enclosure that is at least 3 feet (91.5 cm) tall, 5 feet (1.5 m) wide, and 10 feet (3 m) long. Even with these minimums, it is not a good idea to keep a tortoise in such an enclosure for any extended length of time.

Types of Enclosures

A keeper can make an enclosure out of any number of materials. In this section, we'll discuss some of the more common options.

Plastic Containers A wide variety of plastic containers can be used as an enclosure for a tortoise. Plastic containers are lightweight, durable, and waterproof—all good properties for a tortoise enclosure to have. These containers range in size from small shoe boxes to large plastic tanks used for providing water for farm animals; these are called stock tanks or livestock watering troughs. These stock tanks are also manufactured of galvanized steel. Plastic shoe boxes usually measure about 11 inches long by 8 inches wide by 4 inches high (28 x 20 x 10 cm). They make ideal enclosures for small hatchling tortoises for the first few years. The boxes (and other plastic enclosures) can be used with or without a lid.

Cage Size Guideline

When you are planning out your tortoise enclosure (indoor or outdoor), you can use the following formula as a rule of thumb for the minimum size it will need to be:

Length = 10x

Width = 5x

Height = 3x

The x is the average length of an adult tortoise of the species you plan to keep.

Holes must be drilled in the sides and/or the top if the lid is used. The lid can be useful for when the tortoise gets big enough to climb out. The lid is also useful to maintain a more humid environment, if needed. Plastic sweater boxes usually measure about 21 inches long by 18 inches wide by 7 inches high (53 x 46 x 18 cm). These boxes are useful for tortoises measuring 2 to 4 inches (5 to 10 cm) in length. Some plastic storage containers are designed to roll under a bed, so they usually have wheels on them to make moving them about easier. These containers can measure 3 feet long by 2 feet wide by 10 inches high (91 x 61 x 25.5 cm) or larger. A tortoise measuring up to 6 inches (15 cm) in length can easily be housed in an under-the-bed storage container—although you shouldn't actually keep the tortoise under your bed. These containers can be purchased at most large retail stores and are inexpensive to purchase.

Stock watering tanks can be found in a multitude of sizes and shapes. They can range in size from 3 feet (91 cm) long and 1 foot (30.5 cm) high to over 10 feet (3 m) in length and 3 feet (91 cm) high. The tanks can be rectangular, oval, or round in shape. Stock tanks are water proof and will not corrode. Watering tanks can easily accommodate tortoises up to 12 inches (30.5 cm) in length or perhaps larger depending on how big the tank is. Farm animal feed stores and mail order catalogs are the primary outlet for obtaining these containers. The larger containers can be relatively expensive, but they are very well constructed and will last the lifetime of the tortoise, provided the animal does not outgrow the tank.

One new type of plastic enclosure is bins that are custom-made for keeping tortoises. The custom plastic bins have become popular with the increased interest in keeping amphibians and reptiles. These bins are constructed with partitioned sections, giving the tortoise keeper the chance to provide both a moist

Plastic sweater boxes make fine housing for hatchlings and tortoises less than about 4 inches (10 cm) in length.

and a dry section without the concern of having the moisture spill into the dry section of the enclosure. These enclosures are primarily designed for aquatic chelonians. One section is normally filled with water and has a ramp leading to the dry section. When using these enclosures with a tortoise the ramp actually provides extra exercise and an element of entertainment for both the keeper and the tortoise.

Glass Enclosures Glass enclosures are the next best type of indoor enclosure for indoor use. They are heavier and less durable than plastic enclosures of equal capacity, but they are similarly waterproof. Glass enclosures are readily available at pet stores, although you may need to special-order the size and shape you want. This type of enclosure can be found in a variety of shapes and sizes, but most are oblong or square in shape. The square-shaped enclosures are sometimes called breeder aquariums, and they are designed to provide a large surface area for fish breeding. Breeder aquariums make ideal tortoise enclosures because of the large area, which can measure up to 3 feet square (0.3 sq. m) or more with a height of 1 to 2 feet (30.5 to 61 cm).

The Greenhouse Effect

One important caution to note when using a glass enclosure is that you must be careful to place it so as not to have it in contact with direct sunlight. The glass enclosure will act as a solar amplifier and will quickly overheat the tortoise even in cooler climates if placed in direct sunlight. It should be kept in mind that the sun moves throughout the day, so a shady place in the morning is not necessarily a shady place in the afternoon.

The glass enclosure can also be custom made. The keeper can have the glass cut to size and assemble the panels with silicon adhesive. The edges of the glass do need to have the edges removed using a fine-grained grinding disc or fine-grained abrasive paper or cloth. Plastic molding is also available for covering the edges and corners of a glass enclosure. Custom building allows the keeper more control over the exact dimensions. However, assembling the sheets of glass properly can be very tricky and may not be the best option for the average hobbyist. There are many places where a keeper can obtain a completed custom glass enclosure, but buying a custom-built glass tank can be costly.

Glass enclosures should be open to allow adequate air circulation, easily accomplished by leaving all or part of the top uncovered. You can use a screen top, which will provide a place to rest any necessary lights without significantly hindering air flow.

When some tortoises are kept in glass enclosures they appear to try to get out or try to go through the glass. Some keepers believe that the tortoise is doing this because it can see out. While it is true the tortoise can see out, that is usually not the reason the tortoise is trying to get out. Some tortoises seem to actually enjoy sitting at the glass, as they seem to watch what is going on around them. As a result of the tortoise's being able to see outside it is believed that the tortoise does not sense a physical barrier. This is not the case. All tortoises sense the barrier quite well. Those that try to go through or around this barrier will do so whether the barrier is opaque or transparent.

Tortoises can be housed in large glass aquariums, but these enclosures are heavier and more fragile than plastic ones.

The keeper can always place a tape or painted screen around the boundary of the bottom portion of the glass, but from past experience the author has found this is totally unnecessary.

Wooden Enclosures Wooden enclosures can be the least expensive of the indoor enclosures to provide, but they carry the additional difficulty of properly making the inner surfaces moisture-proof or at least moisture-resistant. This can be extremely difficult if the keeper is planning on housing one of the species that needs a humid environment. The required process of applying the coating properly can be costly and time consuming. Even when applied properly, the coatings applied to the wood to repel moisture do not usually stand up to constant exposure to wetness. As a result the wood enclosure has to be refinished or replaced on an as-needed basis.

Once the wooden enclosure is constructed, the exposed surfaces need to be covered with a moisture-resistant finish. The finish protects the enclosure from rotting caused by moisture from the water bowl and tortoise wastes. If the finish is to be a clear coating but the color of the wood itself needs to be changed, the wood can be stained before the finish is applied.

Stains can be found in many different colors and shades, which can improve the appearance of the enclosure. If a stain is used it must be allowed to dry before the final finish is applied. If the final finish is paint, the application of a stain would not be necessary. It is recommended to apply a minimum of three coats of the finish to the outside of the enclosure and a minimum of 10 coats applied to the inside to ensure adequate protection from moisture. When using paint or varnish each coat should be allowed to dry between coats before the next coat is applied. Each coat should also be lightly sanded with a fine-grit sandpaper or emery cloth. The best choice of finish is an indoor/outdoor coating or a marine finish designed for providing waterproof protection for water craft. The marine finish is a bit more expensive but provides a greater amount of protection.

Paint and varnish are the easiest finishes to apply. They can be applied using a brush, roller, or sprayer. Other finishes that can be used are polyurethane and marine resin. Polyurethane is a good finish to work with because it can be quickly applied if the temperatures are between 70 ° to 80°F (21° to 26.5°C). The polyurethane does not have to fully dry between recoating but should be slightly tacky to the touch which usually takes 30 to 60 minutes. The polyurethane should not be sanded between coats unless it is allowed to fully dry. Marine resin is probably the most durable and waterproof finish, but it is also the most expensive in cost and the most difficult to work with. Allow any of the finishes to fully dry or cure for at least a week in a well-ventilated area before adding any tortoise to the enclosure to be sure any possibly harmful fumes have dissipated.

An important point to remember is that the directions provided by the manufacturer of the finish should be followed in all cases for best results.

Constructing your own wooden enclosure is one of the least expensive options for indoor housing.

The Tortoise Table The most common of the wood enclosures constructed for tortoises is called the tortoise table—so common it gets its own section. The tortoise table is nothing more than a plain rectangular box that is constructed of four sides and a solid bottom. The sides and bottom are fastened using common wood screws. It is often placed on an actual table or—if the keeper is fairly handy—has attached legs to bring it up to a desired height.

The tortoise table is probably the easiest enclosure for average keepers to construct themselves, and it is one of the cheaper options for housing. A hobbyist can construct his own enclosure using very basic tools or can have the pieces cut to the desired sizes and then do the final assembly. Many places that sell and cut wood will also assemble smaller projects for a nominal fee.

These enclosures also are available from specialty pet supply manufacturers and distributors for those keepers who do not have the time or ability to construct a tortoise table. There is some minimal assembly of the purchased table, but there are also clear and concise instructions for assembly. There are also enclosures available from other tortoise keepers who market their building skills to help finance their own hobby. These enclosures are often offered at very reasonable prices and are well constructed.

Bookcases Are for Books, not Turtles

Many keepers try to use bookcases as enclosures. They remove the shelves and lay the case on its back. This is not recommended, because bookcases usually have a thin sheet, often of a composite material, for the back. The thin backboard ends up being the bottom when the bookcase is laid on its back. Once the back gets wet it becomes virtually worthless as flooring; it will warp and quickly fall apart.

Substrate

With the completion of the enclosure, the keeper is ready to add substrate. The substrate (sometimes incorrectly called bedding) is any substance used to cover the floor of the enclosure. It provides the tortoise with traction for walking and may have other functions—maintaining humidity, absorbing wastes, providing a place to burrow—depending on the substrate in question. All tortoises need some type of substrate; do not keep one on a bare-bottom cage.

Sand and Soil Mixtures The most commonly used substrate is a mixture of sand and soil. This can be lightly sprayed to increase the general humidity or can be left totally dry. Because this substrate can be used moist or dry it can be used for any type of tortoise. General purpose play sand and normal potting soil can be used in a 50-50 ratio by volume. Play sand is available at home improvement stores and some toy stores. The sand should be washed and dried to reduce the amount of fine particles, which can irritate a tortoise's eyes and respiratory passages. The soil should not contain any plant fertilizers or moisture-holding particles, such as vermiculite or Perlite—all of these materials can harm a tortoise.

The tortoise table is a popular housing option. It is essentially a large wooden box with appropriate heating, lighting, and other furnishings.

Sand Sand or fine gravel can be used as a substrate in all or part of an enclosure, but it can be untidy when the tortoise walks through water and then on the substrate. The substrate adheres to the tortoise, so the material can be tracked through other parts of the enclosure or through the tortoise's food. If the sand or gravel is lightly moistened this becomes less of a problem. Any type of sand or fine gravel can be used if it is properly washed and dried in order to remove any dust that can be harmful or irritating to the tortoise and the keeper.

Wood Byproducts and Mulch There are many wood byproducts that can be effectively used as a substrate. When light-colored wood is used it actually highlights the tortoise and gives the enclosure a clean appearance. A number of different bark substrates are packaged and marketed for the reptile hobby. These are often blends of different woods and will work for most grassland and forest species.

One example of a wood byproduct substrate is pine bark chips or pine bark mulch—not the same as the pine shavings normally used as small-mammal bedding. This type of substrate is especially good to use when a moist environment is needed. Pine bark chips hold moisture very well when sprayed on a regular basis. Moist chips, however, need to be cleaned out on a regular basis because they attract insects. Changing pine bark mulch on a regular basis should not be a problem, because it is inexpensive and easy to obtain.

Cyprus mulch is similar to pine bark mulch. It can be used exactly as the keeper would use pine bark mulch. Cyprus mulch can be moistened when a humid environment is desired.

Aspen bedding is another useful substrate. It consists of fine wood shavings that absorb moisture well, allowing the keeper to easily spot-clean the enclosure. This type of substrate is suitable for a tortoise that is maintained in a drier environment. Aspen is a light-colored wood that makes the enclosure look attractive when it is used. It is inexpensive and sold in many sizes of packages.

Garden mulches of various kinds are useful substrates for the forest-dwelling tortoises. Be careful to make sure the mulch is organic and free of any fertilizers or dye. The positive aspect of using garden mulch is that it retains moisture very well and provides a good medium for burrowing.

Desert and grassland species, such as the Greek tortoise, can be housed on sand or a sand-soil mixture.

Carpeting Outdoor carpeting is useful with smaller tortoises and tortoises that need to be kept clean while being treated for any medical issues. It is easy to keep clean and sterile while at the same time providing comfort and good footing for the delicate animals. Fine-pile carpeting is recommended so that the chance of the tortoise's trying to ingest the fibers is reduced. Multiple panels of the carpeting can be cut to fit the bottom of the enclosure. This will allow the carpeting to be changed quickly as needed. The carpeting can be cleaned by soaking the soiled panels in a 10 percent solution of bleach and water. The panels must then be thoroughly rinsed in fresh water and brushed to remove any remaining particles.

The carpeting sold for use in reptile enclosures is similar to the outdoor carpeting and will work just as well. It usually comes precut in sizes to fit commonly available aquariums. You may need multiple pieces for an odd-sized aquarium or custom-made enclosure.

Green Astroturf-type carpeting is not recommended, because tortoises are attracted to the green grass-like surface. It is easy for the tortoise to ingest the fibers of this type of carpeting because they come loose easily, and this can cause a life-threatening impaction.

Other Substrates Some substrates that can be used from the outdoors are hay and leaf litter. Hay can be purchased at most animal feed stores. It is inexpensive, and tortoises can feed on the hay between regular meals. The hay that is most commonly used as a substrate is Bermuda hay. This hay has a finer texture and is more nutritious than straw hay. Tortoises also seem to enjoy burrowing into the hay. There are cautions that should be observed when using hay as a substrate. The primary concern is observing how close the hay is to the heat source if one is provided, because hay can catch fire. The keeper should also be careful not to allow the hay to contact any electrical wires in order to also avoid any chance of fire. The final caution when using hay is to not allow the hay to get damp. Any damp hay should be promptly removed to eliminate the chance of having the tortoise consume moldy hay, which could make it sick.

Leaf litter is a good substrate for the forest-dwelling tortoises. It gives the enclosure a natural look in addition to providing good humidity when moistened. To avoid the introduction of unwanted insects and other invertebrates, leaf litter is best collected dry and then moistened. Most forest-dwelling tortoises such as the red-footed tortoise and the forest hingebacks are given added comfort when provided with a moist leaf litter substrate. Leaf litter is also useful as a natural-looking covering over a deeper substrate of soil.

Collecting Substrates

It is not a good idea to use outdoor sources for sand and soil substrates. Some keepers use soils and sands from the outdoors successfully, but the practice is risky: many soils clump up like cement in an enclosure. If you decide to try collecting sand or soil from outside, you should collect it from an unpopulated area where there is no chance of contamination by poisons or any chemical runoff. After collection, the material should be sterilized by steaming or baking.

Furnishings

With the substrate in place, the next step would be to add furnishings to the enclosure. The enclosure can be kept simple by adding only the basic needs such as a hide box and water bowl, or the keeper can get more elaborate with the furnishings.

Home's hingeback and other forest species do well when kept on leaf litter on top of a deeper substrate of soil or mulch.

Hide Box There are many items that can serve as a hide box (often just called a hide), which is a small enclosure within the main enclosure into which the tortoise can retreat in order to feel more secure.

A simple box turned upside down with an access hole cut into the side can be constructed out of wood. A hide made out of wood should be finished the same way a wooden enclosure is (see Wooden Enclosures section).

Square plastic containers make good hides. The keeper can remove the lid and turn the container upside down while cutting a hole in one side to give the tortoise access to the hide. Another option with the plastic container is to leave the lid in place and position the container in the enclosure right side up with a hole cut in the side to allow the tortoise to enter. This is especially useful for creating a humid hide.

Many retailers sell hides such as hollowed-out logs and hollow plastic preformed structures molded in the shape of rocks and logs. These add a naturalistic look to the enclosure. Plastic preformed hollow rocks can also be found at landscaping and gardening centers. These rocks are created for landscaping in order to cover valves and fixtures. Because the rocks are made of plastic, a doorway can be easily cut into the side to allow the tortoise access to the hide.

Water Dish A water dish is one piece of furniture that should be added to every enclosure. This will allow the tortoise constant access to water. The water dish should be placed against one side of the enclosure so the tortoise is sure to find the dish of water as it explores the perimeter of the enclosure. More than one dish can be placed about the enclosure, depending on its size. Placing more than one water dish in a smaller enclosure is not really necessary. As the tortoise becomes familiar with the position of the water dish it will associate the dish with water; the dish can then be placed anywhere in the enclosure. The dish must be low enough to allow the tortoise to easily access the water. You should empty, clean, and refill the dish with clean water daily.

If you do not see any evidence the turtle is drinking, you should soak it in water to make sure it is well hydrated. Once it is certain the tortoise is taking water on its own, the soakings will no longer be necessary. Any plastic container that can contain the tortoise can be used as a soaking vessel. The plastic storage boxes make excellent soaking containers. Be certain when filling the container not to place too much water into the container. The water level should not be higher than the chin of the tortoise to minimize the risk of drowning.

Other Furnishings Other furniture can be added to the enclosure, but the keeper is cautioned not to overdo the decorations in order to allow the tortoise more space to move about. Rocks and logs are good structures that add a natural appeal to the enclosure. In addition to making the tortoise's home more attractive, these objects also disrupt the line of sight and can provide

Humid Hides and Dehydration

A humid hide should be provided to all tortoises, but it is most important with the smaller ones. Doing so helps ensure the turtle is properly hydrated. It is not always possible to provide a humid hide to the larger tortoises because of their size, but their size also makes such a hide less needed. The body volume of large tortoises means they lose less water in relation to size than small tortoises do. Small tortoises, especially hatchlings, can rapidly dehydrate. Giving them access to a humid hide box prevents dehydration.

To create a humidified hide, place a moisture-retaining substrate inside whatever you wish to use as a hide box. An appropriately sized plastic container with an entrance for the tortoise cut in the side works especially well, but any other type of hide will be adequate. The substrate can be coconut husk fiber, sphagnum moss, or paper towels. Dampen the substrate thoroughly. Check the hide every other day or so and remoisten the substrate as needed.

added exercise for the tortoise if properly selected. Disrupting the line of sight is important because it makes the enclosure more interesting for the tortoise by forcing it to be more active as it explores over and around the objects. Another reason for breaking the line of sight is when there is

A tortoise's water dish must be low enough so that it can drink from the bowl easily.

more than one tortoise. Occasionally the tortoises will confront each other to fight or mate. This can sometimes lead to injury if one of the tortoises cannot find an escape route. Visual barriers can provide that escape route.

When selecting rocks or logs as decorations, choose the structures so that they have sloping sides that allow the tortoise to climb up and over, which most tortoises seem to enjoy. Care should be taken when placing structures near the heated basking area, because tortoises sometimes flip over while climbing. If this occurs under a lamp and the tortoise cannot right itself it can become overheated and possibly die. When there is more than one tortoise, one will sometimes flip another over during an altercation. With this in mind it is advisable to place near the basking area a rock structure that will provide a leghold to aid in righting itself.

Large flat thin pieces of stone such as slate, sandstone, or granite can be placed throughout the enclosure. These stones can be used as feeding surfaces, which helps to keep the food off the substrate in addition to keeping the turtle's beak worn down. The stone also aids in the wearing down of the toenails as the tortoise walks or climbs over the stone. Flat stones can be stacked to provide a climbing surface, which not only gives the tortoise more surface area but also provides a good source of exercise. Pancake tortoises, along with a few other species, benefit greatly from the nooks and crannies that can be created by stacking the stones. The tortoises will use these nooks and crannies to seek refuge and sleep. Care must be taken to properly secure the stones so they do not topple and injure the tortoise.

Hot glue guns, silicone rubber cement, nontoxic epoxy, and common concrete can be used to fasten the stones.

Heating

Heating is an essential element when keeping tortoises. Reptiles are totally dependent on the outside air temperature to maintain a good body temperature for proper metabolism leading to good body function. There are a few tortoises that seem to require cooler temperatures than normal, such as some of the Asian mountain tortoises of the genus *Manouria*, and warmer temperatures are not as critical to these tortoises. But those species are more the exception than the rule.

Temperature Range The ideal condition is to provide a temperature range (often called a thermal gradient) so that the tortoise can choose its own temperature depending on its needs at the moment. These needs are going to change, depending on whether the tortoise is just getting up in the morning and preparing to forage or whether the tortoise has just finished

Spider tortoise enclosure furnished with live plants. Tortoises often trample or eat the plants in their enclosure, so they may need frequent replacement.

foraging and requires a good temperature for the digestion process. There is going to be another temperature if the tortoise is slowing down to bed down for the evening. Every tortoise is a unique individual, which is why it is always best to provide as much choice as possible.

Species will also vary in their preference for temperature ranges. Specific temperature ranges will be listed in the accounts for species presented in the final chapters. As a general guideline, most tortoises will do well given a temperature range of 75° to 95°F (24° to 35°C). The keeper should adjust this range up or down depending on the tortoise's preference. If the tortoise is spending all its time at the cool end of the enclosure, it is probably too warm and the heat should be reduced. If the tortoise is spending too much time at the warm end directly at the heat source it is most likely too cool and the heat should be increased. If the tortoise is moving closer to and away from the heat source over the course of the day and seems normally active for its species, the temperature range is most likely a good one for that particular tortoise.

Heat Bulbs There are many types of heat sources that can be appropriate for your tortoise, depending on the particular enclosure that is used. The simplest heat source is the standard light bulb. These bulbs are typically used with a dome-shaped reflector with a ceramic socket. The ceramic socket is recommended because it is not likely to melt or present a fire hazard. It is also recommended to follow the instructions not to exceed the wattage rating normally printed on the socket. This lamp can be suspended above the enclosure or can be clamped to the side of a tortoise table or similar enclosure.

The wattage or power of the bulb is going to determine how much heat is provided by the bulb. Higher-wattage bulbs

Most tortoises thrive when given a temperature range of 75° to 95°F (24° to 35°C).

provide more heat than lower-wattage bulbs. The height of the bulb above the substrate is also going to have an impact on the heat provided. The farther the heat source is away from the substrate the more wattage is going to be needed to provide the proper temperature gradient.

For most applications a simple incandescent bulb will provide sufficient heat. Indoor incandescent flood lamps will direct the heat better than a typical round bulb alone. Outdoor flood lamps and infrared lamps are not recommended for indoor use.

Ceramic Heat Emitters Where light is not needed, a ceramic emitter can be used to heat an enclosure. Ceramic heaters are heating coils housed in a ceramic shell. They screw into a socket, just like an incandescent light bulb. As the name suggests, they provide heat without emitting light. They are useful for heating enclosures at night and for providing heat to the few species that seem to prefer dimmer conditions, such as the forest hingebacks. Always use a ceramic socket fixture for a heat emitter—ceramic heaters will melt a plastic socket.

Thermostats and Rheostats

It is a good idea to use a thermostat or rheostat when using heat lights, heat emitters, and heat mats. A thermostat has a temperature-sensing probe that relays the temperature of the area in which the probe is placed back to the temperature control, which allows the keeper to set a specific temperature. A rheostat does not sense the temperature but allows the keeper to vary the temperature as needed. These devices will help you keep your tortoise's enclosure temperatures within the proper range.

Heat Mats Heat mats are another popular heat source and are highly energy efficient. Heat mats were designed for placement under the enclosure. When used this way, the mat should have a space between the enclosure and the mat to prevent overheating and risk of fire. If there is a wood surface below the heat mat, an insulated mat should be placed between the mat and the wood surface to further reduce the risk of fire. Care does have to be exercised when using heat mats, but they are excellent sources of heat when the keeper takes some minimal precautions. The main precaution to take when using a heat mat is to provide a power source that can be controlled with a rheostat or thermostat. Use only as much power as necessary to provide the temperature range the tortoise needs.

A heat mat can be used inside the enclosure, but it should be protected in such a way so as not to trap heat. One suggestion is to sandwich the mat between two pieces of slate, leaving a space between them. Epoxy or otherwise attach a half-inch (1 cm) spacer onto each corner between the two pieces of slate. Slide the heat mat between the two pieces and put the whole slate and heat mat construction into the enclosure. Be certain to avoid using a wattage that will allow the slate to get too hot. Two pieces of plastic grating similar to that used on overhead lighting fixtures can also be used to sandwich the heat mat. Both of these methods are designed to protect the mat from the tortoise reaching it so the chance of the tortoise's getting harmed is reduced in addition to protecting the wiring and the mat itself from damage by the turtle.

Heat mats can also be placed on the sides or top of the enclosure, but there is great loss of heat when the mat is used in this way. A heat mat can be fixed to the ceiling of a tortoise hide, which will provide a warm place for the tortoise to retreat to at night.

Lighting

Lighting provides a tortoise a stable day and night cycle. There are two basic sources of light—incandescent and fluorescent lights. The incandescent lights can also provide heat, while the fluorescent lighting generates little heat. When using fluorescent lighting supplemental heating is usually necessary.

Ultraviolet B Some incandescent and fluorescent lighting is manufactured to produce ultraviolet B waves, which are invisible to the naked eye. This is the light wavelength that allows the synthesis of vitamin D in the skin of tortoises (and many other

Most wild tortoises bask in sunshine to warm themselves. Heat lamps allow them to perform this natural behavior when housed indoors.

Tortoises

Tortoises require ultraviolet light—either from sunlight or special light bulbs—for normal growth and development.

animals, including humans). Vitamin D is required to allow the body to absorb calcium. This process will be covered in detail in Chapter 3: Feeding and Nutrition.

Most tortoises require some form of UVB. The sun provides it for tortoises housed outdoors. Indoors, you must use artificial sources. When using a UVB light source, there should be no covering between the light and the tortoise. Covering the light with material such as glass, plastic, or fine-mesh screening will filter out some or all of the UVB light waves, making the bulb useful only for lighting and not for a UVB source.

Incandescent Lights Incandescent lighting requires a standard screw-in type housing fixture, which should be made of ceramic to reduce any chance of fire. This is especially important when using a mercury vapor lamp because of the heat such lamps produce. Position the fixtures to eliminate the risk of fire and any chance of harming the tortoise. Normal incandescent lighting can be varied using a rheostat. This could be useful when trying to

Light-Sensitive Tortoises

There is speculation that the UVB radiation can be harmful to the eyes of some tortoises. It is believed that the tortoises such as the yellowfoot, forest hingebacks, and some of the Asian tortoises that normally inhabit forested areas (e.g., *Manouria* and *Indotestudo*) might be sensitive to the intense UVB that is emitted by these bulbs. These tortoises come from habitats that are dimly lit with only patchy and diffuse sunlight. Use caution when using the mercury vapor lamps with these types of tortoises so the eyes are not damaged by the UVB. These species should have plenty of space in the enclosure to get away from the light.

produce certain conditions such as low-level lighting for forest-dwelling tortoises.

The incandescent bulbs that produce UVB are self-ballasted mercury vapor lamps. There are brands packaged for the reptile-keeping hobby, but most mercury vapor bulbs will suffice. An important note when using this type of bulb is that the power into the lamp cannot vary, so they cannot be used with a rheostat, thermostat, or dimmer switch. If the power is allowed to vary, the bulb will shut off internally and will not come back on until the bulb cools down. Mercury vapor lamps come in two forms, spot and flood lamps. The spot lamp puts out a narrow concentrated beam of light; the flood lamp puts out a broader, more dispersed beam of light. It is suggested that the flood-type lamp be used whenever possible because the intensity of the spot lamp also intensifies the heat the lamp produces.

The keeper should be cautious when using a mercury vapor lamp because the lamp can give off enough heat to burn the tortoise. It is for this reason that the keeper should choose the proper wattage and position the bulb high enough so the tortoise is not harmed. In general, a mercury vapor bulb should not be closer than 18 inches (46 cm) to the tortoise.

Fluorescent Lights The fluorescent lamps that produce UVB operate at much cooler temperatures, but they do not put out UVB that is as intense as that produced by the mercury vapor lamps, which makes these bulbs nicely suitable for the forest-dwelling tortoises. The fluorescent bulbs that produce UVB come with labels indicating how much of this radiation they produce. The most common notation is 5.0 and 10.0, with the 10.0 lamps producing higher levels of UVB. Generally speaking, fluorescent bulbs need to be positioned within 12 to 15 inches (30.5 to 38 cm) of the substrate for your tortoise to receive adequate UVB. It is suggested that the fluorescent-type UVB bulbs be replaced every six months because the UVB it produces diminishes with age even though the visible light does not. Mercury vapor lamps also lose UVB output with age, but because the amount of UVB is greater it is not as important to replace the mercury vapor lamps on a time-limited basis.

Fluorescent lighting requires a special fixture you can obtain in any pet supply outlet or lighting outlet. The fixture consists of a socket at each end and internal ballast. Exercise extreme caution when installing or replacing a fluorescent bulb because the ballast produces very high voltage that does not produce a pleasant feeling if contacted. Be sure the power is off when changing a fluorescent bulb. Fluorescent lighting comes in various shapes and sizes, including bulbs that have the ballast contained as part of the lighting unit. These types of fluorescent lights can be used with a standard screw-in socket and are also available as UVB type fluorescent bulbs. Fluorescent bulbs that produce more UVB than any other bulb will soon be available.

Outdoor Housing

It is highly recommended to provide suitable outdoor accommodations for a tortoise whenever possible. There are many advantages and benefits to housing the tortoise outdoors. The main benefit is that it allows the tortoise to lead a relatively natural existence. The space you can offer a tortoise housed outdoors is much greater than most such indoor spaces. Access to the sun is the best source of UVB. The sun allows the tortoise to properly thermoregulate before and after it has fed on the large variety of plants that flourish in the outdoors. For many tortoises, outdoor housing provides the best opportunity to promote the most natural behavior, but it is well understood that providing an outdoor environment in many different geographical locations can be difficult if possible at all.

In most locations falling between the Equator and the 30 degree parallel, keepers should be able to keep their tortoises outdoors most of the year, if not the entire year. Outdoor enclosures constructed in this zone can be simple to construct but can be as elaborate as the keeper desires.

The Basics

The basic outdoor holding pen should be large enough to allow the tortoise ample room to move about. As with indoor housing, the bigger the

Eye Safety

Any light should be positioned so it is shielded from shining directly into the eyes of the viewer. This is especially important when using any UVB-producing bulb. UVB light waves have the potential to damage the human eye with prolonged exposure.

enclosure, the better. The pen should be placed in a location where at least part of it will receive sunlight throughout the day over at least good part of the day. Drainage is an important consideration in areas where there is a large average amount of precipitation. The sides should be high enough to ensure that the tortoise

Red-footed tortoises in a flooded enclosure. Drainage is just one factor the keeper needs to consider when placing an outdoor enclosure.

cannot escape in addition to keeping any unwanted guests from entering the enclosure.

The pen can be considered a walled-off garden if the keeper is going to plant the enclosure with the intention of providing a good variety of natural food for the tortoise. If so, soil preparation and conditioning becomes an important consideration. Grass, weeds, and shrubs are added after the soil is properly prepared. Adding the plants is a critical step not only because it is desirable to make the enclosure aesthetically pleasing but also because the keeper must consider both including a wide variety of edible plants and excluding any toxic species. The furnishings are added to the enclosure last. Once the enclosure is complete there are sometimes going to be additions beyond the basics, such as netting to keep out harmful intruders or heated housing to extend the season in which the tortoise can be kept outdoors. The tortoise is added last.

Size and Materials

The size and type of tortoise will be a large determining factor when deciding on what materials are going to be used for the basic construction. Cost becomes the next largest factor because in many cases the outdoor pen can be quite large and elaborate—and sometimes expensive.

Concrete blocks For smaller tortoises, a simple enclosure can be constructed of concrete blocks. There are blocks that are 9 inches wide by 18 inches long and 3 inches thick (23 x 46 x 7.5 cm) and larger sizes as well. The blocks can be laid end to end and buried roughly a half-inch (1 cm) deep or deeper to prevent the tortoise from tunneling under the enclosure wall. This type of enclosure will suffice for most tortoises up to 5 inches (13 cm) in straight carapace length (SCL). Hatchlings and young tortoises that are kept outdoors on an occasional basis do very well in this type of enclosure. It is recommended that a screen cover be constructed to eliminate the possibility having the small tortoises carried off by a predator.

Another type of block that can be used for larger tortoises is the standard 18 inch long by 8 inch wide by 8 inch tall block (46 x 20 x 20 cm), often referred to as cinderblocks. These are wide enough to be stacked, which allows the wall to be high enough to contain larger tortoises. Walls higher than two rows should not be constructed without the use of mortar between the blocks. Because the blocks contain large empty spaces they are lighter and therefore easier to move and place, and they also provide additional space for plantings if they're filled with soil. Standard bricks or stone can be used with the same results as the cinderblocks, but these materials are more expensive. The main appeal of the stone or brick enclosure is that a well-constructed pen can be very strong and attractive. The brick or stone enclosure would be well suited for the larger tortoises such as any tortoise over 50 pounds (22.5 kg).

Wood You can build a nice outdoor enclosure with various types of wood. The disadvantage of wood when compared to other materials is that it does not last as long if the keeper lives in a moist or humid environment. For this reason, it is suggested to construct the enclosure to facilitate the removal and replacement of those parts that might rot away. Pressure-treated lumber is both easy to work with and relatively inexpensive. It also lasts longer than most other types of wood, meaning it does not require replacement for quite some time. Pressure-treated lumber stamped ACQ; this type is regarded as safe for use with animals. Other types may contain harmful chemicals.

Concrete blocks of various types can be used to make an outdoor enclosure.

As with any other enclosure, a footing should be buried into the ground so the tortoise cannot dig out. Wood can be buried directly into the ground. A brick or concrete footing with the wood on top can also be used.

Support the lumber with wood posts equally spaced along the walls. The support posts should not be farther than 8 feet (2.5 m) apart; positioning them closer together makes the walls that much stronger. Rails can be placed between the posts with slats attached to the rails, or the posts can be slotted to allow long boards to run horizontally between the posts. With the second method there is no need to secure the boards, which eliminates the need for nails or screws. The nice aspect of using treated wood is that it does not have to be protected from the elements as would untreated wood, but treating it with paint or varnish would only extend the life of the wood.

Chain-Link Fencing Chain-link fencing is another type of material that is frequently used to construct a tortoise enclosure. Enclosures made from this material are very durable. The materials can be expensive, but the fencing will never have to be replaced. This type of fencing comes in a 2-inch (5-cm) mesh and a 1-inch (2.5 cm) mesh, which is sometimes called tennis court fencing. The smaller mesh is recommended for the smaller tortoises.

The fence consists of posts with rails supported at the top from which the chain-link fencing is hung. The bottom of the fencing should be buried at least 6 inches (15 cm) into the ground or 12 inches (30.5 cm) in the ground for those tortoises that actively dig.

The bottom of the fencing can be shaded to prevent the tortoise from seeing out. The shades are plastic strips that are threaded between the links either horizontally or vertically. The height of the shade will be determined by the length of the tortoise and should be at least one and a half times the length of the tortoise. If the tortoise is not inclined to constantly try and go through the fencing, the shade can be omitted. The main advantage of the

Wooden enclosures are relatively inexpensive and easy to make, but they may not last as long as those made of other materials.

Outdoor enclosure made of chain-link fencing. Note the heated hiding area and the mulch substrate suitable for humidity-loving species.

chain-link fence is in areas where there is heavy rain, especially on sloped areas. The fencing allows the rain to easily run off without the concern of proper drainage or damage to the enclosure materials.

Soil

Before any furnishings are added to the finished enclosure it is recommended to make sure the soil is adequate to support the plants you want to include. This might require soil preparation. It is always a good idea to have the soil tested, which takes all the guesswork out of knowing what nutrients or physical preparations it might need. Most local garden outlets either do the testing themselves or know the soil type of the area to the point that they know what needs to be added. Soil preparation is a very important step in setting up an outdoor enclosure, and it is best to do this before the tortoise is added, because it is very difficult if not impossible to do so afterward. In most case nutrients and organic matter have to be added unless the keeper is lucky enough to live in an area with rich soil.

Any local plant nursery is the best source of guidance and information when soil preparation is an issue. Plants are then added after the soil is prepared. It cannot be stressed strongly enough how important good soil preparation is. The soil preparation is for the benefit of the plants, but it will save a great deal of time and trouble to install any electrical wiring for

Dealing with the Big Boys

There are no exceptional problems with housing average-sized tortoises outdoors. However, there needs to be special concern when keeping the larger tortoises, such as the Aldabra or sulcata, in an outside enclosure. Careful thought needs to be given if a keeper is thinking of maintaining any of the larger tortoises. This is especially true in cooler climates. They are going to require very large enclosures and over-wintering facilities, which would include a warehouse or barn as either winter or all-year housing. The farther you go from the Equator the more challenging this becomes, because these tortoises become very large and require a great deal of space. Additionally, they are very strong and can dig extensive burrows. Use sturdy enclosure walls, such as cinderblocks reinforced with cement. You should sink the enclosure walls at least a foot (30.5 cm) beneath the ground to prevent the tortoise from tunneling out of the pen.

lighting and heating once the soil has been conditioned and before any other plants or furnishings have been added.

Furnishings

Once any needed electrical wiring has been installed, the plants and furnishings can be added. Not all tortoises do well in a lushly planted enclosure. Some tortoises come from drier areas or rockier areas. It might be necessary to provide a layer of substrate that is more natural to the tortoise on top of the prepared soil. Sand and gravel or a mixture of the two can be spread over all or part of the enclosure to a depth of at least 2 inches (5 cm). Any of the desert- or arid-dwelling tortoises, such as the Greek tortoise and Russian tortoise, would do well in such an enclosure. Larger rocks and logs can be added at this time. This not only provides an appealing outdoor enclosure but also provides obstacles, which break up the monotony of the enclosure. These structures also provide cooler and moister microhabitats that these tortoises benefit from when they hide under or near them.

The enclosures housing tortoises that come from more moist habitats, such as the red-footed or any of the forest-dwelling tortoises, can be covered with leaf litter or any kind of mulch. The enclosures can then be extensively planted. The same structure as previously mentioned can also be added. This type of enclosure can also be carpeted with grass or sod. The grazing tortoises, such as the leopard and sulcata, can also use this type of enclosure. Care must be taken when using commercial sod because this type of grass usually has a nylon backing that helps hold the grass together so it does not fall apart. This nylon backing can make it difficult for tortoises to be able to nest. It might be better to plant these enclosures with durable grasses.

Plants

There are thousands of plants suitable for planting within a tortoise enclosure—far too many to discuss in detail in a book of this size. Which plants you can use will depend on your climate and soil conditions. Your local gardening stores will have many useful varieties, and you can order seeds and young plants from catalogs and online vendors.

Any of the plants recommended as food in Chapter 3 might possibly make good plants for the enclosure. Note that most of the edible plants will need frequent replacement. Also, be aware that the many plants that have edible parts may also have toxic parts. One example of this would be the plants in the nightshade group, including tomatoes, potatoes, and eggplants.

Many shrubs and small trees make great plants for tortoise enclosures. One caution is that there has been little research into which plants are toxic or edible to tortoises or other reptiles. It's good rule of thumb that plants listed as toxic for other pets, such as dogs and birds, may be toxic to tortoises. However, given that

An outdoor tortoise table is useful for housing hatchlings and small species.

tortoises have different physiologies from most other pets, these lists should not be taken as definitive. There also exists the possibility that some plants might be toxic to some species of tortoise but not others.

Here is a short list of plants known to be safe for tortoises:
- cactus (spineless varieties)
- clover
- day lily (not the similar tiger lily)
- ficus (figs)
- forsythia
- geranium
- grape
- hibiscus
- hollyhock
- lavender
- mulberry
- rose
- rose of Sharon
- waxleaf
- yucca

Clover and a mix of grasses are suitable for planting in an enclosure housing any of the grazing species, such as the Greek tortoise.

Electricity and the Outdoor Enclosure

It is important to know what the building codes in your area are before installing electrical wiring in your outdoor enclosure. Most outdoor wiring is covered in building codes. An electrically skilled keeper might want to do the job himself, but it is recommended that an electrician take on this particular task if it is to be done properly and safely. There are some inherent hazards when working with electrical power, especially when used in outdoor applications. Whether the electricity is installed by the keeper or a professional electrician, it is important that any wiring be protected by a ground fault circuit interrupter (GFCI, also commonly called a GFI). A GFCI greatly helps to protect the animal and the keeper from accidentally getting electrocuted. The GFCI works by automatically and very swiftly, almost immediately, cutting off the power if it notices even very tiny changes in the flow of the electrical current, as in the case of a short circuit.

Heating

Not all tortoises are going to be able to stay outdoors naturally full time and will require supplemental heating. The easiest way to provide this heating is by placing a heated structure in the enclosure. The size of the structure can be as small as a dog house or as large as a small cabin. This is going to depend on the size of the enclosure and the size and number of the tortoises in the enclosure. Any housing should be well insulated to reduce the cost of the heating. The doorway of the house should have cover, such as a movable door flap. This can be made of wood or plastic. The door cover will also reduce the cost of heating. Tortoises quickly learn how to use this entrance. The heating can be provided by a heat mat or overhead heating in the form of a ceramic heater or incandescent lamp. An infrared lamp is not recommended, because of the risk of the tortoise's getting burned. As with indoor heating, any outdoor heaters should be controlled by a rheostat or thermostat.

Water

Standing water, such as a water dish or pond, is one method of providing water. Another way to provide added moisture is through the use of a sprinkler or misting system. In those areas such as desert climates these are not only suggested but might even be necessary to maintain certain tortoise species. Even when using sprinklers or misters, provide a water bowl or a small pond.

Many tortoises seem to enjoy soaking and even swimming. Therefore many keepers like to provide a larger water bowl or small pond. Care should be taken if a cement pond is provided. The keeper should make sure the cement is properly cured or sealed. Regardless of the pond's composition, its sides should have a slope that allows the tortoise easy access and good footing so the tortoise can enter and exit the pond without any hazard.

Rinse out and replace the water in the bowl daily. This may be difficult if using a small pond. In that

Red-footed tortoises using the heated structure within their enclosure.

case, it is best to use a hose with a nozzle that produces a strong jet of water. Using the jet, you can blast any debris out of the bowl and then use a more gentle spray to refill it.

Cleaning and Maintenance

No matter the type of enclosure being used, it will need to be cleaned periodically. Clean enclosures are essential to the health and well-being of your pets. It's a good idea to inspect the

Cold Frames and Greenhouses

In cooler climates, the use of a cold frame or greenhouse can be employed to house tortoises outdoors or to extend the season in which tortoises can stay outdoors. The cold frame is an enclosure with a glass cover, and a greenhouse is a house made of glass or plastic. These houses can cover the entire outdoor enclosure or only a part of the enclosure, with a door allowing the tortoise to enter and exit as it wishes. The one caution when using such an enclosure is to be careful in the placement of the structure and not place it under any trees where there is a risk of falling limbs. If such a structure is used to cover the entire enclosure it is recommended that the housing be constructed of a material that allows UV through. Normal glass filters out beneficial UVB. If such an enclosure is used in warmer climates, the keeper should be cautious of overheating. Avoid overheating by providing proper ventilation.

Outdoor enclosure with a cold frame.

cage furnishings, enclosures walls, etc., for wear or damage while performing cleaning chores.

Cleaning Indoor Enclosures

Indoor enclosures are spot cleaned as needed by removing any waste. This is easier if the waste is allowed to dry out, but a paper towel or pet scoop (such as a cat litter pan scoop) can be used just as well. Remove the waste as soon as you see it.

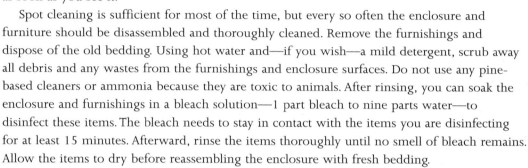

Spot cleaning is sufficient for most of the time, but every so often the enclosure and furniture should be disassembled and thoroughly cleaned. Remove the furnishings and dispose of the old bedding. Using hot water and—if you wish—a mild detergent, scrub away all debris and any wastes from the furnishings and enclosure surfaces. Do not use any pine-based cleaners or ammonia because they are toxic to animals. After rinsing, you can soak the enclosure and furnishings in a bleach solution—1 part bleach to nine parts water—to disinfect these items. The bleach needs to stay in contact with the items you are disinfecting for at least 15 minutes. Afterward, rinse the items thoroughly until no smell of bleach remains. Allow the items to dry before reassembling the enclosure with fresh bedding.

If you use some type of carpeting as a substrate, it can be soaked in bleach and then in clean fresh water to remove the bleach. The carpeting should then be allowed to properly dry out before being replaced.

Clean and Maintaining Outdoor Enclosures

If the outdoor enclosure is set up properly, it becomes more or less self sufficient, with the exception the plants becoming overgrown. Some plants will have to be trimmed on occasion. The keeper may need to replace some plants—not all plants will survive. Minimal waste cleanup is required because the waste becomes fertilizer for the plants. However, if the tortoise droppings are drawing undesirable vermin, you will need to be more vigilant about their removal. Larger tortoises require more frequent spot cleaning because of the large size of their waste. The wastes do make a rich fertilizer and can be composted.

Water dishes should be scrubbed regularly to remove algae. This can be done using a stiff nylon bristle brush. One nice aspect of a well setup outdoor enclosure is that it dramatically reduces the workload of tortoise keeping because natural process take care of much the maintenance.

Geochelone gigantea

Chapter 3

Feeding and Nutrition

The most important aspect of tortoise keeping—aside from keeping the animal in a suitable habitat—is feeding and nutrition. Many tortoise keepers find this one of the most confusing areas of their hobby because it is such a broad and abstract topic having so many differences of opinion as to what is the proper method of providing that nutrition and what is considered improper or bad nutrition. What the keeper needs to understand is that there are so many differences of opinion for a reason, and that reason is that there is no single one way of providing good nutrition for the many different species of tortoises in captivity. The basic suggestion to the keeper following this guide is to learn as much as possible about nutrition and do follow-up research to that information.

Tortoises are largely herbivorous and need a varied plant-based diet.

Tortoise Metabolism

The most important aspect of tortoise physiology as it pertains to nutrition is that tortoises are cold-blooded. This term is slowly being phased out because the blood is not really cold. Today, the terms poikilothermic or ectothermic are more widely used. These two terms are more accurate because they mean the organism is dependent on its surroundings to regulate its body temperature. This is opposite to a homeothermic organism, which can regulate its body temperature internally, as mammals can do.

Because tortoises are ectothermic their metabolism is going to vary depending on their outside environment. In captivity they should be provided with a good temperature range so the tortoises can choose to self-regulate their body temperatures according to their needs. There is normally a spread of roughly 20 degrees Fahrenheit (11° C) in the proper temperature range for most tortoises. For example, most species of *Testudo* will do well with a temperature range of 75° to 95°F (24° to 35°C), while sulcatas and Aldabras do well with a temperature range of 80° to 100° (27° to 38°C). Tortoises kept outdoors self-regulate their body temperature, depending on the outside environment and the supplemental heat that is provided.

A tortoise's thermal needs are going to be different depending on whether it just woke up from a rest period or it is getting ready to forage for food. Once it has eaten, its metabolic needs are again going to change, so the tortoise is going to seek out a different temperature. The normal cycle for this activity is that the first thing in the morning, then again in late afternoon, the tortoise will preferentially seek out higher temperatures. In captivity, there is likely to be an ideal growth situation because the tortoise will not be limited to access its preferred temperatures at certain times of day (or even the year). In the wild the tortoise has a limited choice based on seasonal changes in addition to geographical location, so activity level and growth are going to vary dramatically over the time of day and time of the year.

Tortoise metabolism also varies from species to species. Some tortoises, such as some of the Asian species including *Manouria*, are active at lower temperatures. Other tortoises, such as some of the *Testudo* species, are inactive at warmer temperatures. Tortoises have individual metabolisms, similar to the differences you might see in individual people. The behavior of both the species and individuals within the species is one metabolism-influencing factor that is not mentioned often. Some tortoises are more aggressive feeders than others and as a result will usually grow quicker. Other tortoises have different schedules of temperature regulation, which appear to be personality based. All of this will influence a tortoise's growth and development.

Providing too little heat will cause the tortoise to slow down to the point of being forced into a perpetual rest period until temperatures return to favorable conditions. The tortoise does this because its metabolism slows down due to the low temperature, which does not allow the tortoise to move about to eat and digest. All tortoises will respond in the same manor to this condition. This is seen by some as the tortoise's hibernating, but it is not a true hibernation and is commonly referred to as brumation because the temperature of the tortoise

Temperature and Digestion

The internal temperature of a tortoise will determine the metabolic rate of that tortoise. This in turn establishes the pace and efficiency at which nutritional components are processed. In short, warmer tortoises eat more and process that food faster and more efficiently than cooler tortoises.

The metabolism of a tortoise is affected by the temperature, and tortoises will not eat if they are too cold.

has fallen to the point that it can no longer function properly. If the temperature were to go in the other direction where conditions are too hot, the tortoise would seek out an area where it can avoid any tissue damage from heat. The tortoise will then go into a rest mode called estivation, during which it will bed down in an area where the heat is low enough to prevent tissue damage. The tortoise will remain there until more favorable conditions return. Both of these points will be covered further in the tortoise health section.

Hydration

It is apparent how important heat is in the biology of a tortoise for it to maintain the temperatures needed to properly metabolize the nutrients needed for it to develop good health and grow in good form. Anytime heat is added there is an equal loss of hydration in both the animal and the environment. This is where the second most important factor in nutrition comes into play. If the shell is disregarded it would not be hard to see that the tortoise is made up mostly of water. This is why hydration is the second most important factor in the biology of tortoises. These two factors are equally important, because without either of them none of the biological processes can take place properly. In the wild many tortoises can go without water for long periods only because they have adapted over time to deal with the harsh environments that nature provides for them. In captivity the tortoise is at the mercy of the tortoise keeper. This is why it is so important for the keeper to make sure the tortoise is properly hydrated.

Two types of hydration are recognized: internal and external hydration. Internal hydration is the more important of the two types. It is the water that the tortoise takes in that keeps the tortoise well hydrated. External hydration is the water in the environment (in the form of humidity and moisture); external hydration helps maintain the tortoise's internal hydration by reducing moisture loss that occurs through normal respiration. Tropical tortoises normally have a humid environment, which reduces the problem of moisture loss through respiration—but may also mean that these species are less resistant to dry conditions, being that they are not adapted to cope with low humidity. Arid and desert tortoises have adapted to their particular environment by retreating into burrows during times of drought or low water availability.

In captivity internal hydration is provided by the use of a drinking water container and/or regularly soaking the tortoise. If the tortoise is seen to be using the water container it is not necessary to provide regular soakings. Another method of providing water for the tortoise to drink is by spraying the tortoise and enclosure. Some tortoises can collect the sprayed water by raising their hind end and drinking the water that accumulates on their back and drips forward towards the head. Tortoises will also lap drops of water off the enclosure wall

Hydrating Small Tortoises

It is extremely important to make certain that smaller tortoises such as hatchlings and species that are small by nature either use their water source regularly or are soaked on a regular schedule. Hatchlings should be soaked once a day or every other day. Soaking for larger tortoises can take place once or twice a week. The smaller species of tortoises would include the Egyptian tortoise, some of the hingebacks, and the star tortoise. These tortoises are extremely susceptible to renal failure if proper internal hydration is not maintained.

and furnishings. If this method is used the enclosure and furnishings should be allowed to dry between mistings to reduce the accumulation of mold in the enclosure. This should not be a concern with forest tortoises.

The Importance of Variety

All tortoises have the same basic nutritional needs. This is a very important point because in the wild tortoises have adapted to their ecological niche by evolving to hunt and consume certain plants and organisms to fulfill those nutritional needs. Forest-dwelling tortoises are thought to consume larger amounts of carrion and fruit than grassland tortoises because that is what is available to them. For the purpose of this guide the common idea of certain tortoises preferring certain foods is going to be followed, but the fact that certain tortoises prefer a certain food does not indicate the food is required. In other words, just because a tortoise prefers to feed on something does not necessarily mean the tortoise needs to consume that food. Remember that a particular food can be replaced by a nutritional equivalent. We do this every day when we currently provide food for any captive tortoise. The foods we provide are not the same as the turtle would find in the wild, so it is a substitute. It is very difficult to tell a keeper exactly what a tortoise actually needs nutritionally. Every species of tortoise is different and every individual in that species is going to have different nutritional needs, as explained earlier. For this reason the best a keeper can do is to provide as much variety as possible if using a green-based diet or to use a trusted complete commercial diet that can be supplemented with dark leafy greens along with hay or grasses and some fruit.

Protein

Protein is probably the most important nutrient and also the one most commonly blamed for physical problems seen in tortoises. Too much protein is said to be the cause of a physical malformation called pyramiding, which is a bumpy or conical appearance of the shell. The cause of pyramiding is hotly debated, because there is more than one factor influencing

Hatchling tortoises are especially prone to dehydration, and soaking them daily is recommended.

Providing the Natural Diet (or Not)

Some conflict comes into play when discussing nutrition because many keepers believe that providing a natural diet is the only way a tortoise should be raised and that every other diet is wrong. This is not bad in theory, but it is basically impossible unless you live within your tortoise' natural range. The next best way to provide a truly natural diet is to observe the type of tortoise you are keeping in its natural habitat and record what the tortoise consumes over many years (because plant availability is going to vary from season to season and year to year). Neither of these options is very realistic for most keepers, so we do the best we can in providing a varied and nutritious diet for our animals.

this shell deformity. Too much protein is also blamed for many other developmental maladies. The main problem with this understanding is that no one really knows what amount actually is too little or too much protein. Many experienced keepers suggest limiting protein by feeding a high-fiber/low-protein diet. Inexperienced keepers who follow this advice commonly end up with a malformed tortoise or a tortoise that is not growing properly, because protein is extremely important for proper growth, development, and other physiological functions. Proteins not only form structural building blocks but also carry out specific functions in the internal processes within all living things. It is for this reason that it is suggested that the keeper not focus on limiting protein intake and just make sure to provide a highly varied and properly formulated diet.

The widespread advice about feeding a high-fiber/low-protein diet seems to be an overreaction to the feeding of canned cat or dog food to tortoises, which used to be a common practice. These foods contain animal byproducts, including red meat, entrails, and animal fats. Tortoises are considered herbivorous because they have evolved to consume and process mostly plant material. The digestive system of a tortoise is very similar to that of a rabbit or horse, mammals that are considered hindgut fermenters. In hindgut fermenters, the stomach is relatively small and crude, with little digestion taking place there. Most of the breaking down of food is done in a modified large intestine with the aid of aerobic bacteria. This type of digestive system has evolved in animals that eat mostly nutrient-poor foods (usually grasses) frequently throughout the day. Their digestive systems process food quickly and more or less constantly. There is not much opportunity to absorb nutrients, so the tortoise's body has become efficient at using the nutrients it does obtain.

A sulcata helping itself to some aloe vera.

This is not to say tortoises cannot consume lean meat and other animal protein. Most tortoises will consume this kind of material in the wild on an incidental basis. Redfoots, hingebacks, Asian brown tortoises, and some other forest-dwelling tortoises are known to consume more animal matter than the average tortoise. While these species still need a primarily herbivorous diet, some animal protein—such as earthworms and insects—in their diets seems to be beneficial.

In captive tortoises, the damage seems to come from the high content of fats and acids normally found in canned processed pet foods. Protein content in a tortoise diet should not be a consideration if the tortoise is limited to a varied plant-based diet. For this reason it is suggested that the keeper focus on a high-fiber diet but not place emphasis on limiting protein intake.

Fiber

The majority of a tortoise's diet is going to be fiber by nature. Fiber is the indigestible plant material—mostly cellulose in plant cell walls—that is consumed by the tortoise. The main purpose of fiber is to retain moisture as an aid in the digestion process. In tortoises, fiber is partially digested with the aid of beneficial bacteria in the hindgut; the cellulose is converted to fatty acids and other nutrients.

Vitamins

Vitamins are organic compounds that are not produced by the tortoise in significant amounts, so they must be obtained in the diet. They have numerous and varied roles in bodily functions. Any deficiency in a vitamin can lead to disease and possibly death. Conversely, an overdose of a vitamin can lead to poisoning and death. That is why it is important to exercise extreme caution when supplementing vitamins.

Vitamin Supplementation

If you decide to include vitamin supplements in your turtle's diet, it is important to note that different tortoises are going to need different ratios of vitamins. A red-footed tortoise is not going to require the same amount or ratio of vitamins as would a leopard tortoise.

Currently there is a vast assortment of vitamin supplements on the market from which a tortoise keeper can choose. The recommended approach to using vitamin supplements is to choose those that have been available for the longest amount of time. They have usually have been available long enough that if there was any problem from using them it would have been apparent by now. Always use supplements that are made specifically for reptiles. The best vitamins have vitamin A in the form of beta carotene, a precursor to actual vitamin A. This last point is important because it is very easy to overdose with vitamin A. When it is provided in the form of beta carotene, the tortoise's body can make it into vitamin A as needed, reducing the risk of overdosing.

Variety Is Key

Variety in the tortoise diet is a big key because many keepers tend to focus on one food or a very limited range of foods. This gives the animal a very incomplete portion of all the nutritional components required for good development. It appears that there are no real clinical studies which have determined exactly how much of which nutrients a tortoise actually needs. When you factor in all the different species and individuals of those species it becomes an impossibility to know for sure exactly how to feed tortoises. The best bet is to provide the tortoise with the widest variety of foods possible. This helps ensure that it is getting all the nutrients it needs.

Do not put liquid vitamins in the water. They promote bacterial growth, and some tortoises do not like the taste and will not drink the water.

When supplementing vitamins, be cautious for the first few weeks of use and watch how the tortoise reacts to the supplements. It is very easy to oversupplement, so it is best to start off with a very light dusting on the food. A salt shaker serves well as a vitamin dispenser. Consult with other keepers on what supplements they use and what have been the results of their use. If feeding a good varied diet or formulated diet it should not be necessary to add anything to the diet. However, adding a vitamin supplement once a week should not do any harm if the keeper feels the diet is not enough. Once a diet has been used for some time the keeper might consider cutting back on the vitamin supplementation if it is felt to be unnecessary.

Minerals

Minerals are the final member of the most important four components of tortoise nutrition. Minerals are elements that are needed to maintain and support normal physiological functions in the body of the tortoise. Minerals are broken down into three categories: macrominerals, microminerals and trace elements. Macrominerals are those minerals that are required in large amounts. In humans, this amount would be anything above 100 milligrams per day. Two examples are calcium and phosphorus. Microminerals are minerals that are required below that level. Examples of microminerals are chromium, copper, and zinc. Trace elements are required in amounts less than microminerals. It is thought that trace elements are required in minute amounts, but the exact amounts are not known. Additionally there is debate over whether some of these minerals are needed at all or whether other minerals not now considered trace minerals really should be considered so. Examples include nickel and strontium.

Speke's hingeback and the other hingebacks are more omnivorous than most other species and should be fed insects, worms, and other forms of animal protein.

Calcium and Phosphorus

Calcium and phosphorus are two extremely important minerals that work together in many bodily processes. They are critical for proper formation of the bones and, most notably, the shell. It needs to be noted that calcium and phosphorous interact in the control of many of the physiological functions of the tortoise body. Calcium is used not only in the formation of bones and the shell but also throughout the body as a chemical regulatory mechanism. The calcium ion is widely used in many body functions including muscle contractions, nerve impulses, blood clotting, and activation of enzymes, among other things.

For optimal health, a tortoise's diet should contain more calcium than phosphorus. A ration of two-to-one calcium to phosphorus is ideal. This does not mean you need to know the exact chemical composition of your tortoise's food. What it does mean is that you must supply a diet that is very rich in calcium. Obtaining enough phosphorous is usually not a problem, because it is a major element in plants.

It was mentioned that vitamin and mineral supplements should be used sparingly. There is one exception to this suggestion: calcium supplementation. In addition to needs for calcium and phosphorus that other animals have, turtles have a unique need: the shell. A tortoise's shell is mostly made of these two elements.

Most nutritional disorders that occur in tortoises involve calcium. It is for this reason it is suggested that calcium be added at each feeding. The most easily accessible and useable form of calcium is calcium carbonate. This can be found in the form of fine lime power or cuttlefish bone. When using cuttlefish bone it is suggested that the hard backing be removed for smaller tortoises. This backing can be sharp when it breaks away and can cause harm to the tortoise. Cuttlefish bone can be scraped or ground into a powder and then sprinkled on the tortoise's food. When this form of calcium is use in conjunction with natural sunlight it is very difficult to overdose.

Dietary Parasite Control

Fiber—sometimes called roughage—also acts as a scrubbing aid in the digestive tract. It helps keeping the parasite load down in tortoises in the wild and cleans out the tract. If tortoises are being are being maintained outdoors, this is something that should be considered. Your tortoise will pick up internal parasites no matter how diligent you are in maintaining a parasite-free outdoor area, but the roughage will usually keep the parasite load to a minimum.

There are forms of supplemental calcium that contain vitamin D3, which is essential for the metabolism of calcium. Care must be taken when these supplements are used because when supplements with D3 are used there is the added risk of overdosing by allowing the body to metabolize too much calcium, which can lead to calcium's being deposited in

Many keepers use cuttlefish bone as a calcium supplement. Use a knife to scrape it over the tortoise's food.

the tissues and joints of the tortoise. The benefit of using these supplements is that UVB would not be required for the metabolism of the calcium. This could be beneficial for tortoises maintained indoors where UVB lamps are not used—although you really should be using a UVB lamp.

Tortoises, especially fast-growing juveniles, are very susceptible to bone and shell deformities. The culprit is almost always a problem with the levels of calcium, vitamin D, and/or phosphorus in the diet. Many bodily processes depend on there being a certain concentration of calcium in the bloodstream for normal function. This concentration is controlled by the interplay of several hormones. When this level drops, the thyroid gland releases one hormone that stimulates the release of calcium from the bone while at the same time increasing calcium retention by the kidneys (i.e., less calcium gets lost in the urine). With the aid of vitamin D, the uptake of calcium ion by the intestine is also increased. When blood calcium concentrations return to normal, the thyroid gland releases a different hormone that signals the kidneys and intestine to reduce calcium ion uptake while at the same time causing calcium deposition in the bones.

Proper calcium metabolism is one of the major reasons that hydration is so important. If the kidneys are blocked due to salts or urates, the kidney does not allow the replenishment of calcium. The needed calcium is then removed from the bones, leading to a weakening of the skeleton. This is commonly seen in hatchlings and is sometimes noted as failure to thrive, which is usually not the case.

Creating a Tortoise Diet

By and large, tortoises are herbivorous animals, and the keeper should provide his tortoise with a varied diet comprising mostly leafy greens. The types of plants tortoises eat in nature depend largely on their habitat and secondarily on the season and other factors. The grasslands species, such as most *Testudo* and leopard tortoises, feed mainly on grasses. Desert species, such as sulcatas and Egyptian tortoises, feed on grasses, succulents, cacti, and aloes. The forest species, such as red-footed tortoises and Asian brown tortoises, feed on a wide variety of leafy plants, along with significant amounts of fruits and mushrooms. The dietary information presented here applies generally to all tortoises. You should tailor the diet you offer to the species of tortoise you are feeding.

Plants in the Enclosure

The easiest and safest way to provide a greens-based diet is to have a well-planted outdoor enclosure. This will allow the tortoise to choose what it needs, and this usually results in a healthy and great-looking tortoise. Tortoises seem to know what they need when they are given the choice, so it is important to plant the enclosure well. Use as many different varieties of plants as possible and observe what your tortoise eats. An outdoor enclosure also provides the added benefit of some native flora (a.k.a. weeds) springing up, which will only add to the variety available to the turtle.

Today there are outlets that sell seeds and seed mixes for tortoises in addition to seeds of wild plants that are normally consumed by animals, such as rabbits. Many weeds are used in natural salads eaten by people, so seeds are available for salad plants, which is nice because tortoises benefit from the same diet. Once again the key is going to be to

Macro and Micro

All of nutrition is broken down into two major categories, which are called macronutrients and micronutrients. Macronutrients are those nutrients that make up the bulk of the tortoise body. These nutrients include protein, fat, carbohydrates, water, and macrominerals such as calcium. The micronutrients are the vitamins and minerals that make up a minor portion of the actual makeup of the body but are essential for the normal cellular processes. Without the micronutrients the tortoise would not survive or at the very least would develop physical problems.

provide a variety that will hopefully cover all the nutritional bases. If it is not possible to provide a large variety of plants, be sure to research the nutritional value of each plant and try to have as little duplication of nutrients as possible.

In well-planted enclosures tortoises will forage for most of their own food.

The list of plants you can grow in a tortoise enclosure is effectively almost limitless. One way to get some ideas is to research the edible plants grown in your area. You can also find out what local tortoise keepers plant in their enclosures. The following is a short list of plants accepted by a wide variety of tortoises for the keeper to use as a starting point:

- alfalfa
- chicory
- clover
- dandelion
- grape vine
- grasses
- lavender

- mallow
- mints
- mustards
- nasturtium
- plantain and other plantagos
- thistle

A tortoise that is allowed to graze or browse on its own will usually give the keeper an indication of what it will or will not eat. If a tortoise is observed eating a plant that is toxic to mammals, the keeper should not panic. Many reptiles can consume without harm plants that are toxic to mammals. However, if there are any doubts to the safety of a certain plant, it is better to be safe than sorry: remove the plant.

Collecting Plants

Tortoises that are kept in captivity are not always going to be able to be kept outdoors. Those tortoises that are not kept outdoors or are kept in an outdoor enclosure that is not well planted are going to need to have some or all of their food provided for them.

Collecting greens should not be a problem for most people, but there will always be the tough question of what kind of greens are safe to feed. Any dark leafy green is usually safe to feed the tortoise, but if there is any question it is advisable to have the plant positively identified before using it as food. Some of the more common weeds keepers feed their tortoises are any of the plantain family, dandelion, and milk thistle. The best source of information for identifying local edible weeds is through a plant nursery or natural history museum. The use of a guide that lists the local flora is also a good source for identifying plants.

Once the keeper has a general idea of what to collect and feed the tortoise, there are many good areas where these plants can be found, starting at the keeper's own yard and the yards of neighbors. Be cautious of fertilizers, herbicides, and pesticides; never use them in areas you collect tortoise food from, and make sure your neighbors refrain from their use as well. Some of the best places to collect weeds are the local school yards and parks. Herbicides are usually not used in these areas because of the presence of children, but the keeper should always ask to be sure. Collecting weeds from the roadside is not recommended due to the emissions from the vehicles and runoff from the roads.

Tortoises will sample any plant that springs up in the enclosure, adding to the variety in the diet.

Store-Bought Plants

It is not always possible to grow or obtain greens from the outdoors. During unproductive periods the same greens that are planted outdoors can be planted indoors or in a greenhouse and harvested as needed. For those who are not good at raising plants or do not have the space to grow plants indoors, there is always the grocery store or farmers market as a source of food for the tortoise. Whenever

Feeding and Nutrition

Mushrooms

Some tortoises, such as the hinge-backed tortoises, seem to have a preference for mushrooms. Other species, including the flat-tailed tortoise and red-footed tortoise, also seem to enjoy mushrooms. Include edible mushrooms in the diet of these species whenever possible. Although some turtles—notably box turtles (*Terrapene* spp.)—consume mushrooms that are known to be deadly to humans, it is safest to feed tortoises only nonpoisonous mushrooms.

feeding grocery greens, it is advisable to use a complete vitamin supplement because, while they are acceptable, they can have a limited nutritional value.

When using grocery greens the same cautions apply as when selecting greens from the outdoors. Special care should be given when selecting grocery greens because many of them are very high in oxalic acid and glucosinolates (see section: Plants to Limit or Avoid). Any of the dark leafy lettuces such as romaine, green leaf, red leaf, and the dark leaves of iceberg lettuce are acceptable as food for the tortoise. Mustard greens, collard greens, dandelion greens, arugula, and escarole are also good choices. Cactus pads are available at Hispanic grocery stores and are very high in calcium. Many groceries carry prepackaged greens, which contain a good mix of lettuces and other greens. When feeding these mixes, be careful that the ingredients do not include too many plants that are best not to feed to tortoises.

Legumes, such as string beans and snap peas, can be fed in limited amounts as part of a varied diet. Fruits and berries are acceptable foods for all tortoises in limited quantities. Melons and other fruits with high moisture content can be fed occasionally to tortoises. Forest tortoises can eat these fruits more regularly; these tortoises seem to be able to handle the digestion of these fruits better than other species. Red-footed tortoises seem to feed heavily on fruit in the wild, so keepers of this species should often include fruit in the diet. Frozen mixed vegetables are acceptable on a limited basis, such as those times when all other options are not available. Allow frozen vegetables to thaw to room temperature before offering them to your pet.

Plants to Limit or Avoid

There are certain plants that should be avoided or fed very sparingly. The plants at the top of that list are high in oxalic acid. Oxalic acid binds with calcium to form calcium oxalate, an indigestible salt. This acid robs the body of calcium and is one of the main culprits behind kidney damage in tortoises. If there is too much calcium oxalate or not enough water to flush the salt, it can damage the kidneys and also form stones in the bladder. There is not much information on the oxalic acid concentration of wild plants, but on the list are the plants of the genus *Oxalis* and related plants; they are very widespread, with more than 900 known species. The common names of these plants include wood sorrels, false shamrocks, and sourgrasses . Store-bought greens that should be fed in a limited amount because of the high oxalic acid content are spinach, chard, rhubarb, watercress, parsley, and beet greens.

Another group of chemicals that causes problems in tortoises are the glucosinolates, which are found in plants of the *Brassica* group. These chemicals are implicated in the formation of goiters, impaired thyroid function, and liver damage. These plants are commonly called goitrogenic plants. They include cabbage, kale, bok choy, brussels sprouts, broccoli, cauliflower, rapini, and related plants.

Oxalic acid and the glucosinates are selected out for mention because they are common causes of health problems in tortoises.

Romaine lettuce and other leafy greens are excellent additions to the diet.

Animal Matter

Forest-dwelling tortoises are going to enjoy occasional animal matter in the form of insects, such as caterpillars or crickets. Pre-killed baby mice can also be used on occasion for these species—but while the tortoises seem to really enjoy them, it is not at all pleasant to watch. Snails and slugs are also good sources of animal matter, but care should be taken when collecting these mollusks to be sure they are not taken from an area that might have been poisoned by a gardener who wishes to get rid of them. Some tortoises, especially the forest hingebacks, relish earthworms, which are fairly high in calcium. It is acceptable for all tortoises to take an incidental bit of animal matter if the tortoise happens to come upon it and consume it.

Commercial Tortoise Diets

Not all tortoise keepers have the time or the resources to feed a totally green-based diet. Others might like to supplement the diet with something more nutritionally complete. For those keepers there is the option of feeding a manufactured diet formulated by animal nutritionists specifically for tortoises. These diets are usually distributed by pet supply distributors and are available at pet stores that sell reptiles.

Tortoise Escargot

Tortoises will occasionally consume snails, slugs, pill bugs, and other invertebrates they happen across in their enclosures. This should be of no concern to the keeper, because this is normal behavior for those tortoises that choose to do so. Incidental eating of these animals occurs on a regular basis for many of the different tortoises in the wild.

Some formulated diets have been around for over 30 years and have been used by zoos and large collections for a long time. During recent years these diets have started becoming popular among private tortoise keepers. Those commercial diets that have been available for many years can be trusted based on their longevity in the market and the results obtained by tortoise keepers feeding the diets. Others are relatively new on the market and should be used with caution because of this newness. One positive point regarding the newer products is that they benefit from hindsight of the results of the products that have been on the market for some time. So their makers have seen what could be improved on with the older products. This is not to say that the older products are using the same formula they have been using all along. The good manufacturers constantly

Tortoises feeding on a commercial diet supplemented with calcium powder.

monitor their products through their customer input and adjust the formulation of their products accordingly.

Keep in mind that formally educated animal nutritionists direct the formulation of these products. This ensures that the tortoise keeper is getting a diet created based on the most up-to-date information.

Currently there are two basic forms of these manufactured diets: processed pellets and hay-based pellets. The processed pellets are in a highly digestible form that looks similar to a paste when wet. These diets are usually grain- and soy-based products with a good amount of fiber. Additionally, they contain all the vitamins and minerals in a general ratio that will ensure the proper development of a tortoise. Because these products are so nutritious and easy to digest, the keeper must carefully control the amount fed. The manufacturers normally recommend a percentage of the tortoise body weight to be used as a guide to the dry weight of the food that should be fed daily. These diets can also be fed ad lib once or twice a week.

Growth of the tortoise can be rapid on this diet, but the growth is normally smooth (i.e., no pyramiding or other deformities seen) if all the environmental conditions are correct. The keeper can always reduce the amount being fed if he is not comfortable with the rate of growth. Feeding can always be increased if the keeper feels the growth rate is not adequate.

These diets can be used on all tortoises because all the needed nutritional components are readily available to any species of tortoise to digest. While many of these diets can be fed as stand-alone diets, they should be supplemented by those foods that are normally consumed by

Yummy Stones

During foraging tortoises often ingest stones or some of the substrate. No one really knows why they do this, but there is speculation that it is an attempt to take in minerals. There should not be any concern with the tortoise's ingestion of those items. If they went in, they will come out of a healthy, well-hydrated active tortoise. Watch to make sure they do not take in too much substrate or an object that is too large, because this does happen on very rare occasions.

individual species to add variety and possibly make up for any possible unknown deficiency. For example, hinge-backed tortoises and some of the Asian tortoises consume mushrooms and snails in the wild, so these items should be part of the captive diet of those tortoise species. Another example is the feeding of fruit to red-footed tortoises and some other forest-dwelling species. For other tortoises, the addition of dark leafy greens is recommended as a filler and fiber as a supplement on the days or times the diet is not being fed. The keeper can also use grass clippings or hay as a supplement.

The other pellets currently on the market are hay- or grass-based diets, manufactured mostly in response to keepers calling for a commercially available grass-based natural diet. This type is not a complete diet, and it is not marketed as such. Vitamins and minerals are added to most, but care should be exercised when using such diets because they are going to be lacking in some nutritional elements. Some manufacturers have taken it a step further to create a grass- and weed-based-pellet, but these diets are still not complete. Most of them currently on the market are relatively recent, but they do appear to be good products. The grass-based pellets would be a perfect match as a supplement to the previously mentioned complete diets. These diets are not formulated but are processed and compressed grasses and weeds. The ratio of the nutrients is going to be highly variable and unknown because of the material used and the way it is processed.

The main benefit of using a complete formulated pellet diet along with a hay- or weed-based pellet diet is that it takes all the guesswork out of tortoise nutrition. The tortoise keeper knows the tortoise is getting the proper nutrition it needs. With a green-based diet, the tortoise nutrition is going to be hit or miss, with the keeper hopefully providing all necessary nutrients from a variety of plant material. It is for this reason a pellet diet is recommended for the novice tortoise keeper to begin with. The keeper will not have to be concerned that the tortoise is not getting the proper nutrition it needs as he learns about the plants and the nutrients they contain. If the keeper wishes to feed a green-based diet, the pellet will give the keeper time to learn which weeds and greens to collect and how much to feed of each while knowing the tortoise is already getting what it needs.

The pellets in a pellet diet be moistened prior to feeding to make them easier for the tortoise to ingest. Once the tortoise has finished eating the moistened pellet diet, any remainder should be removed because it can spoil and harm the tortoise if the food is ingested.

How Much to Feed

The quantity of food fed is yet another one of those greatly debated topics among tortoise keepers—and it really doesn't need to be if certain things are considered. All debates start with what a tortoise does in the wild. Although we are concerned with pet tortoises, the study of a species and how it lives in the wild is a good starting point.

Tortoises are exposed to the harsh conditions that nature presents them with. These conditions include cold weather and possibly drought, floods, and other extremes. These conditions lead to reduced food supply and long periods of inactivity. The rate of growth of a tortoise in the wild is going to vary and is going to be dramatically different from that of a tortoise in captivity. The quantity of food being fed to the tortoise in captivity is the reason for the difference, along with the usually constant environmental conditions provided by the keeper. Even the tortoise that is kept outdoors usually has supplemental heating. Even though the tortoise is kept outdoors and exposed to the elements, it has better

It is safe to supplement your tortoise's diet with grass clippings, and many tortoises will enjoy this.

condition than if it was in the wild on its own. For the captive tortoise the only foods that should be limited are those that are nutritionally rich and easily digested. There is no reason a varied green diet should be limited, which is especially true if the tortoise is outdoors and foraging during its periods of activity.

Tortoises normally begin foraging early in the morning when they first awaken and then again in the late afternoon before bedding down for the evening. Forest-dwelling tortoises, such as some of the hinge-backed tortoises, are occasionally nocturnal feeders, but this behavior is more the exception than the rule. In areas where it is unbearably hot during the day some species will also occasionally feed at night if they are not estivating. These periods of activity are the best times to offer food. If a green-based diet or hay is offered it will stimulate the tortoise to forage if the food is scattered about. The food can be left out as long as it does not stay wet and spoil.

Let your tortoise show the quantity of food it needs. The amount of food a tortoise eats is based on the temperature, along with the individual needs of a given animal. In most cases, if a tortoise is active it is feeding. Because of this, overfeeding

Indoor tortoises should be fed daily, and the keeper should adjust the quantity of food depending on the needs of the individual turtle.

It Eats What?!

Some tortoises have the nasty habit of consuming their own feces and the feces of other animals. The technical term for this is coprophagy. Why they do this is any keeper's guess, but the popular theory is that they take the already digested material to extract even more nutrition from it. Rabbits have a similar habit, if they are given the opportunity. Remember that the tortoise, like the rabbit, is a hindgut fermenter, so most of the digested material is wasted before it can be used. This habit might actually be beneficial to the tortoise. It is totally up to the keeper whether to allow the tortoise to do this, but the majority of tortoise keepers do not go out of their way to discourage their tortoises from eating feces. There is a concern about the risk of cross-contamination by internal parasites when the feces come from other animals, but that risk is likely no greater than the concern caused by a tortoise's eating weeds that the birds have defecated on.

should not be a concern most of the time. This might be an issue for tortoises kept indoors and/or fed primarily a pelleted diet. You can feed an indoor tortoise daily as long as the quantity is limited. Keep a close eye on the tortoise's weight and cut back if it is getting too heavy. If the tortoise is outdoors and eating the plants in the enclosure, you can provide supplemental greens, hay, and pellets, along with more limited quantities of other vegetables and fruits daily or a few times weekly.

Final Word

Nutrition is probably the most difficult section to understand in all of tortoise keeping. It is a complex and controversial topic because there are no specific answers to most if not all of the questions that are raised. The best you can do is to learn as much as you can on this topic and see what works for your tortoise in your situation. Every single individual tortoise is different, and no two tortoises are going to require the exact same thing. Each diet is going to have to be adjusted to accommodate each individual. This can be as simple as adjusting the quantity or as complex as preparing a specific diet for each individual. A tortoise keeper must strive to provide the best possible diet to the tortoise; a tortoise fed an excellent diet rewards its keeper with a long healthy life.

Geochelone elegans

Chapter 4

Breeding and Reproduction

Keeping tortoises quite often leads to getting so involved with the hobby that hobbyists often want to take the tortoise-keeping experience beyond keeping just one or two animals as pets, and that can lead to wanting to breed them. To some tortoise fans, the life cycle of a tortoise is not complete until the tortoise breeds and reproduces. However, attempting to breed tortoises must be done with careful consideration of the steps—and possible setbacks—that come with this endeavor.

The Key for Success

Good housing and nutrition lay the basic groundwork for tortoises that are not only healthy enough to breed but also willing to breed. Providing tortoises with excellent care is the best way to ensure that they will breed. If all the conditions are just right, you may be lucky enough to go from tortoise keeper to tortoise breeder.

Before You Get Started

In order for breeding and reproduction to take place many elements need to come together under just the right circumstances. The most important factor is the presence of a male and a female tortoise. Making sure your tortoises include both sexes might sound easy to achieve, but the sex of most tortoises is not easily determined at an early age, and some tortoises are difficult to sex even as adults.

The tortoises then need to be healthy enough to breed. The pair needs to be in perfect health and have the nutrient reserves to produce the eggs and survive the stressful process. This is especially true of the female. The pair of tortoises then has to be compatible. If the tortoises are not willing to breed, there is no reason to be concerned with the rest of the process.

Once the tortoises do breed, the odds of producing viable youngsters are not very good most of the time. Eggs are not always produced, and those that are produced are not always going to be fertile—and if they are fertile they are not always going to hatch. If and when hatchlings do emerge, they are at their most fragile state . The hatchlings do not always survive, but the vast majority normally does, only to require more diligent care than an adult tortoise needs. All of these points will be addressed further in this section of the guide, but it needs to be stressed that breeding tortoises is a process that carries no guarantees through every step no matter how diligent and well prepared a keeper is.

Determining the Sex of a Tortoise

Determining the sex of a hatchling tortoise is nearly impossible to do. There are some tortoise breeders who incubate the eggs to hatch out tortoises that are very likely to be a given sex (see section: Temperature-Dependent Sex Determination. When obtaining a pair of tortoises from such a breeder, the keeper can start out with a male and female hatchling. If you want to start with hatchlings and can find only ones of unknown sex, you should buy at least five to be almost certain you have at least one male and at least one female. Be sure that you are committed to raising up this number of tortoises before you embark on a breeding project.

Surgical Sexing

A relatively new method to sex hatchlings is gaining popularity. It is a minimally invasive veterinary procedure that involves the use of an endoscope—a small fiber optic camera. A small incision is made in the pocket just in front of the hind leg and the camera inserted into it. The body cavity is filled with an inert gas to allow room for the camera. With the aid of the camera, the veterinarian can see the sexual organs, which are attached to the kidneys. The testis and the ovaries are very distinguishable organs even in a one-inch (2.5 cm) tortoise. This procedure is not particularly invasive—although it might seem so—and it is 100 percent accurate. Many tortoise conservation programs use this procedure with excellent results. It is available to the average tortoise keeper, but it can be costly. If a keeper is interested in some of the more expensive tortoises, the benefit could outweigh the cost.

External Differences

It is always going to be less expensive to start a breeding project with hatchlings, but the keeper is not going to be guaranteed a male and female tortoise. Although fully adult, breeding-size tortoises are more expensive, a prospective breeder can be more certain of their sex. Most tortoises are sexually dimorphic, meaning the male and the female have different characteristics. As a general rule the male tortoise is going to be smaller than the female and have a longer and thicker tail. The vent of a male tortoise usually is on the tail out beyond the edge of the plastron, while that of a female will be close to the plastron's edge. In many species, the plastron of the male is concave, while that of the female is flat.

The carapaces of the males are also less domed than those of the females. There are exceptions, as in the case of the pancake tortoise, in which both male and female are flat. and usually of equal size for equal-age tortoises. The female-larger-than-the-male rule is inapplicable in Aldabra and Galapagos tortoises as well, the male in those cases usually being

In most species, including the flat-tailed tortoise, adult females are larger than adult males.

Why Are Wild-Caught Tortoises Harder to Breed Than Captive-Bred Ones?

There are some things a tortoise keeper can do that could increase chances of success in getting the tortoises to breed. In the past tortoises taken out of the wild were the only tortoises available. Some wild-caught tortoises were not only difficult to acclimate into captivity but also nearly impossible to establish well enough to breed. If the tortoises were acclimated into captivity, breeding still did not occur in many cases, because the potential mates had imprinted on environmental cues of which the keepers were unaware. Wild tortoises are at the mercy of climatic changes, anything from cold or hot weather to rainy or dry seasons. Through natural selection, tortoises have adjusted their breeding cycle to conform to those conditions—producing eggs at times when the conditions are most likely to allow them to hatch and the resulting young to survive.

Wild-caught tortoises look for certain cues before they attempt to breed. If they do not perceive the cues, usually they will not breed. One of the more common and obvious cues to induce breeding in tortoises is hibernation. Many species will breed upon emergence from hibernation. Hibernation is one of the few breeding cues that can be easily duplicated in captivity.

Other cues that induce breeding are more difficult to reproduce in captivity. They could be any number of environmental factors: changes in humidity, changes in rainfall, changes in hours of daylight, etc. Breeding cues will be different for different species and may even vary within a given species over the range of that species. To breed tortoises, the cues to induce breeding have to be reproduced by the keeper, and they often have to be reproduced within a certain time frame. Wild-caught tortoises seem to have internal clocks that tell them when they should look for the cues. It is for this reason that it is very difficult to breed wild-caught tortoises. Captive-bred tortoises have more or less adapted to breeding in captivity and are less finicky about the conditions in which they will breed.

Some wild-caught tortoises are available, but they should be left to the more experienced tortoise keeper. The only advantage to trying to keep and breed wild-caught tortoises is that many species are not currently or commonly bred and only wild-caughts are available.

larger than the female. Where exceptions to the general sex determination guides occur, those exceptions will be pointed out in the discussions of individual species later in the book.

Some tortoises are easier to sex than others, even as they mature. Tortoises of the genus *Testudo* can usually be sexed at 3 to 4 inches (7.5 to 10 cm) SCL. Marginated tortoises are an exception; they need to be at least 6 inches (15 cm) SCL. In all cases the male is going to be easier to sex at an earlier age than the female, which means that you can be more certain you have a male than you can be certain you have a known female at the younger ages.

Male (left) and female (right) marginated tortoises. In this species and most others, the male has a concave plastron and long thick tail. The female has a flat plastron and much shorter tail.

Breeding Age (or Size)

Starting with hatchlings and raising them up to breeding size will of course take longer than starting with turtles of breeding size. Breeding in these animals is more dependent on the size of the individual than on its age. Many tortoises that can reach breeding size in as little as four years, but in the larger tortoises such as the Aldabra and Galapagos tortoises, the eventual adult size results in a longer time until these species can breed. Aldabra tortoises are usually about 21 years old before they produce eggs. This might sound like a long time unless you consider that that the species's breeding size is not reached until the tortoise weighs about 250 pounds (113 kg).

Leopard tortoises and sulcatas can reach breeding size in as few as four years. Breeding size for those species is 10 to 14 inches (25.5 to 35.5 cm) SCL. Egyptian tortoises can attain breeding size in a similar amount of time, but they only need to attain a size of 4 inches (10 cm) SCL. The sizes noted are for the female of the species. The males are smaller in size than females when reaching sexual maturity.

The breeding sizes listed are possible of attainment only when the tortoises are kept under ideal conditions and growing more rapidly than what is thought to be normal in nature. To put it in perspective, both the Egyptian and leopard tortoises would normally not reach the size of sexual maturity until they were roughly 10 years old or more. The main point is that sexual maturity is based on size and not age.

Hibernation

Many tortoise keepers believe that hibernation is a necessity for the species known to hibernate in nature. Hibernation is an adaptation by the tortoise to survive unfavorable environmental conditions that would otherwise kill it. A tortoise would not hibernate if environmental conditions were favorable for survival throughout the year. You do not need to hibernate your tortoise unless breeding is your goal. Additionally, never hibernate a species that does not hibernate in nature—it is highly unlikely to survive.

Hibernation in Nature

As reptiles, tortoises are totally dependent on the temperatures available in their environment to provide adequate heat for metabolism and bodily functions. When it gets cold their metabolism slows down, and if it slows enough they will be unable to move and will likely die. In the wild tortoises instinctively seek the warmest place they can find that will keep them from freezing. Most often this place is a burrow that extends below the frost line of the soil. The cool temperatures keep the tortoise in a stupor. When conditions become warm enough, the tortoise will begin to move and seek out warmer locations—usually by basking. Many species commence breeding shortly

Male (right) and female (left) leopard tortoises showing differences in the plastron.

Russian tortoises and most of the other *Testudo* species hibernate during the winter. In captivity, hibernating these species often stimulates breeding.

after emerging from hibernation. This is an adaptation that ensures that conditions are favorable for egg incubation and the survival of the hatchlings. Hibernation therefore often serves as a reproductive cue.

Hibernation carries risk with it. A tortoise can freeze or starve to death during hibernation. The tortoise's immune system is weakened when the temperature is low, exposing the animal to disease. The hibernating tortoise also is vulnerable to predators, such as rats and mice, which can chew on the tortoise. Many tortoises in nature do not survive hibernation.

Hibernation in Captivity

While hibernation often stimulates reproduction, it is not a necessity for the good health of the tortoise. Tortoises will live long and healthy lives even if they are never hibernated. Some tortoises breed without hibernation, but success is much more likely with hibernation. The keeper does have to weigh the risks versus the benefits. Hibernation is a simple process but if attempted incorrectly the tortoise may not survive.

The most important thing to do before hibernating a tortoise is to make sure it is in excellent health. The tortoise should have good weight and be free of parasites. It may be a good idea to take the turtle to the veterinarian for a checkup just to be sure there are no underlying health issues that could worsen during hibernation. If a tortoise's health is at all in question, it should not be hibernated.

Hibernation Consultation

The description of hibernating tortoises is a general explanation of the process. It is highly recommended that you seek out the guidance of a fellow tortoise keeper who lives in your particular area. A local keeper is sure to have useful information and experience to share regarding hibernating tortoises within your specific climate. You should be able to find a friendly and knowledgeable local hobbyist through your local herpetological society or via the Internet.

Outdoor Hibernation The best means of hibernation is to allow the tortoise to control its own actions. This can be done by providing a place to hibernate outdoors such as a pile of hay or mulch surrounded by bricks or other enclosure. You can also dig a hole down below the frost line and fill this hole with leaves, grass clippings, and sand or soil. Any hibernation area you provide needs to be in a well-drained area and in such a place that there is no chance of going below freezing.

As the temperatures get cooler, the tortoise will feed less often and eventually stop eating. Before it starts to dig into the hibernaculum (burrow in which an animal hibernates), it will evacuate any remaining material from its digestive tract. This will prevent the partially digested food from spoiling inside the gut during hibernation. At this point it will dig a hibernaculum, close up the opening, and rest there until warm weather returns.

Indoor Hibernation If the tortoise is kept indoors or if the local climate does not get cold enough for outdoor hibernation, you will need to hibernate the tortoise artificially. The first step is to slowly lower the temperature over the course of a couple of weeks.

The temperature needs to be dropped to a point where the metabolic rate of the tortoise is low enough so the tortoise can survive through hibernation without using up its body reserves. A safe temperature for hibernation is 41° to 46°F (5° to 8°C). If it gets any higher the tortoise runs the risk of starving to death, and if it goes lower there is the risk of freezing or frost damage. Many keepers use a cellar, unheated garage, or tool shed for hibernating their tortoises at the proper temperature. Those living in warmer climes may have to use a modified refrigerator. To modify a refrigerator for hibernation, you will need to remove some of the insulation so that it holds a steady temperature in the desired range of 41° to 46°F (5° to 8°C). You should monitor the temperature with a digital thermometer for at least a week before you place tortoises inside it so that you know it will stay in the safe range. Make sure there is adequate ventilation in the refrigerator.

You will need to make your tortoise an artificial hibernaculum. Provide the turtle a box partially filled with hay, cloth, or shredded paper. This box can be left in the enclosure or placed wherever the temperature will hold the proper hibernation range.

When the tortoise is hibernated in an artificial environment it should be checked and weighed on a regular schedule. A weight loss of up to 10 percent is acceptable over a two-month period before there is cause for concern. When taking the tortoise out of hibernation the temperature should be raised gradually to allow the tortoise to properly acclimate. While weighing the tortoise, check it for signs of ill health, and if any are present, stop hibernation and take the animal to the veterinarian.

At the end of the two- to three-month hibernation, gradually raise the temperatures up to normal. Once the tortoise is moving about the hibernaculum, you can move it back to the enclosure and resume feeding. You should soak the tortoise daily for a week or so after it comes out of hibernation.

Estivation

Tortoises will estivate if the temperatures get too hot. In captivity, there is no reason to induce estivation on purpose, but if the keeper lives in a climate where temperatures get extreme, he needs to make provisions to allow the tortoise to get out of the heat. Temperatures above 110°F (43°C) are cause for concern.

Outdoor Breeding

Breeding success is most likely accomplished when you are housing tortoises outdoors in a climate similar to their natural one. If the climate is different, a breeder can still be successful if he creates a similar climate and habitat within the enclosure, for example with supplemental heating and careful attention to plantings. The tortoises must be allowed to remain undisturbed if they are expected to adapt to

Male tortoises will spar with each other during the breeding season, as these angulated tortoises are doing.

Breeding and Reproduction   85

Species That Hibernate

Those species that are known to hibernate are those that occur above the 30 degree north latitude and below the 30 degree south latitude. They include the following species:

- **Bell's hingeback (southern populations)**
- **desert tortoise**
- **Greek tortoise (European populations)**
- **Hermann's tortoise**
- **leopard tortoise (southern populations)**
- **marginated tortoise**
- **Russian tortoise**

the outdoor conditions successfully and be inclined to breed. This is made easier if a keeper lives in an area that has a similar climate as does the tortoise's natural range.

As was pointed out earlier, providing a proper temperature is a task that becomes harder to deal with the farther a keeper is away from the Equator. Supplemental heating can help but can only go so far. Breeding tortoises outdoors for warm-weather species becomes less likely or more difficult the farther you move away from the Equator. This will obviously limit the keeping of larger tortoises, such as the sulcata or Aldabra, to the warmer climates if there is any intention of breeding the animals. It is almost impossible to breed those species indoors.

Indoor Breeding

Some tortoises are well suited to indoor reproduction. Keepers have more success reproducing those tortoises indoors than they would if the tortoises were kept outdoors, regardless of the geographic region. Some good candidates for indoor breeding are the Egyptian tortoise, the flat-tailed tortoise, and the other smaller tortoises from Madagascar.

It would appear that those tortoises require strict climate control in order to get them to breed. The greatest breeding success achieved with the flat-tailed tortoise has been accomplished by those keepers who provide a distinct wet and dry cycle, with the temperature remaining relatively constant. The tortoises are allowed to dry out for a few months, and then they are sprayed down regularly for a few months. This wet season seems to trigger breeding and egg laying. This is just one example of how a keeper might be able to induce breeding in a species. Those tortoises that are found in forest or rain forest climates seem to be those most likely to respond to a wet dry seasonal change to induce breeding. Spring to early summer in the northern hemisphere and fall to early winter in the southern hemisphere is when mating will usually take place and will take place throughout the breeding season.

Courtship and Mating

When males are sexually active they seem to always want to breed. The female will sometimes run away with the male in hot pursuit. If the male catches the female he will usually ram her until she sits still. This can sometimes lead to the male's harming the female. The marginated tortoise is one species in which the males are well known for inflicting severe damage during the courtship process. It is not unheard of for a male marginated tortoise to crack a female's shell by the ramming her. Many male tortoises will also bite at the female's legs in an attempt to get her to sit still. Sometimes the biting will draw blood. Occasionally the male will flip the female over or the female will flip the male over.

   If the female tortoise is receptive she will stop moving and even raise her hindquarters to allow the male access for mating. The male will then mount the female with his front legs on the female's shell and his head above hers. The male tortoise usually has his mouth open as he emits a series of vocalizations

A male interested in breeding will follow a female around and try to corner her, as this male Egyptian tortoise is doing.

Breeding Cues

A pair of tortoises usually requires some kind of external stimulation to induce breeding; such stimuli are called external cues. With captive-bred and captive-raised tortoises this is sometimes as easy as dropping the temperature for a period or providing a dry and wet cycle. Tortoises that are kept outdoors for extended periods of time usually adapt to local seasonal changes and develop a rhythm in sync with them.

during mating. This is amusing because not many people envision a tortoise as being vocal, but they are extremely vocal; in fact, the voice carries for some distance regardless of the size of the tortoise. The vocalizations can range from a squeak to a coo to a honk to a groan depending on the species. Mating can last from a few minutes to more than 30 minutes, but when the male is done or the female decides to move on, they part company and go their separate ways. The obvious observation is that there is no emotion involved.

As a rule it will take more than one breeding for a female tortoise to become gravid (pregnant with eggs). The male has to do more than just to inseminate the female; the female needs to be ovulating at the same time, and this sequence is not always in sync. Although the chances of fertilization are going to increase with the increased frequency of breeding, there are still no assurances that eggs are going to be produced even if breeding is observed.

Nesting and Egg Laying

If the male was successful in fertilizing the female, eggs can be produced in roughly 30 days for most tortoises but usually get deposited later than this after a successful mating. It is reported that tortoises can retain sperm for up to five years, which means that a tortoise can produce viable eggs five years after successfully mating. This is not a normal occurrence but is possible.

Some tortoises can lay eggs roughly every 30 days throughout the season, but laying just one or two clutches of eggs is more the norm for most tortoises. Tortoises can deposit from one to over 30 eggs, depending on the species and the size and health of the female. Most tortoises normally deposit two to seven eggs in a clutch. In the temperate climatic zones tortoises normally deposit eggs in the spring and the fall but can deposit throughout the active time of the year. Tortoise from tropical climes may lay eggs at any time of the year but usually do so in sync with the rainy season or other local climactic changes. Many females seem to develop a pattern of depositing eggs at nearly the same time every year and at approximately 30-day intervals if they lay more than one clutch.

Finding a Nesting Site

When a female is ready to dig a nest for her eggs, she will begin to pace the perimeter of her enclosure. She will pace in a restless and hurried fashion as she looks for a suitable place to nest. As the tortoise runs its rounds searching for a good nesting site, she will occasionally stop and sniff the ground.

The tortoise will usually choose a nesting site where the nest will get the most warmth. This could be in the sun, but this is not always the case. What is interesting is that when a particular female chooses a certain nesting site she will usually choose that same nesting site or a very nearby place on subsequent nestings.

Digging the Nest

Once a suitable nesting site is selected for depositing the eggs the tortoise will start digging and will not stop until the task is done. If the substrate is too dry, the female will moisten it with fluid from her bladder as needed throughout the digging process. The nest is usually flask-shaped, having a relatively small opening on top that expands into a larger chamber the deeper the tortoise digs. The depth of the chamber is as deep as the farthest the female can reach with her outstretched hind legs.

Egg Laying

The tortoise will then deposit the eggs; the actual depositing of the eggs looks like a long, labor-intensive process. As the tortoise passes the eggs a viscous fluid surrounds the egg, which allows it to slowly drop, thus preventing the breaking of previous eggs. This is

Male radiated tortoise ramming a smaller female as part of courtship. This behavior is common in tortoises.

Breeding Makes Them Cranky

During breeding season it is not only the opposite-sex interaction that the keeper should be concerned about. Male-to-male interactions can be just as hostile as male-to-female interactions, and they are often worse. Female-to-female hostilities are usually not as bad as male-to-male, but occasionally they do occur, with an equal amount of damage to the combatants. That is one reason to place logs or rocks into an enclosure—they break up the line of sight between combatant turtles. If either of the tortoises can get out of the other's line of sight, the aggressor usually will lose interest and move on. If fights continue, you may have to move the individuals to separate enclosures.

true in most cases, but occasionally some eggs are cracked as they fall and hit each other. The cracks are usually minor, so no action is necessary to address them. During the laying process female tortoises seem to be in a trance-like state, oblivious to their surroundings.

When the tortoise is finished laying, she starts covering up the nest. You can move the female at this time in order to remove the eggs for artificial incubation. Place the eggs into a suitable container and take them to the incubator. The tortoise can then be placed back onto the nest, where she will continue to cover it.

It is important to try to catch the tortoise in the nesting process because if you don't see the female nesting it is nearly impossible to determine where the nest is. After covering the nest the tortoise will scratch the surface of the surrounding area and move the material over the nest to camouflage the actual nest. If the female is allowed to complete the nest before the eggs are removed, it is important to be very careful in removing the dirt from around the eggs. This task should be done by hand if at all possible to avoid damaging the eggs. If you know that the eggs have been deposited within a few days of being dug up, there should be no concern with rotating the eggs. If the age of the nest is not known, however, you should try to maintain the eggs in the position in which they were found. When an embryonic tortoise starts to develop, it does so in a specific position, usually at the top of the egg. In the beginning stages of development the tortoise is very delicate, and rough handling can tear the embryo away from the yolk sac, resulting in death; the eggs should be handled very carefully. A good idea is to mark the top of the eggs in pencil so you can be sure you aren't turning them.

Providing a Good Nesting Area

It is important to provide a good nesting site to gravid female tortoises. There should not be much concern with tortoises that are maintained outdoors if the enclosure was set up properly. That said, adding a sandy area or keeping an area slightly more moist than the rest of the enclosure will help ensure there is a suitable nesting area. For indoor setups, the tortoise can be maintained in an enclosure with a substrate deep enough for proper nesting. The substrate will need to be a few inches deeper than the tortoise is long.

Nesting boxes can also be used for smaller tortoises. The boxes are filled with a moist substrate that allows the tortoise to dig a proper nest. Sand, vermiculite, coconut husk (also called coconut fiber and coir), and sand/soil mixes are common choices depending on the species of tortoise and keeper preference. The nesting box can be placed in the enclosure or can be a separate box such as a large plastic container. When a female is observed trying to nest, she can be moved to the nesting box, where she will usually continue nesting. Shredded newspaper can be balled up and placed in the nesting box to simulate plant cover, which can make the nesting tortoise feel more secure.

Tortoises will occasionally deposit eggs haphazardly on the ground for some unknown reason. Some believe that the tortoise does this to evacuate unneeded bad eggs. Some females that have never been with a male will do this on an infrequent basis; in this case the eggs are infertile. However, you should remember that females can store sperm, so if the female has mated within the last few years there is a chance the eggs are viable. The eggs should be incubated and not discarded, although the chances of their hatching are not very good.

Mating marginated tortoises. In nearly all tortoises, the male is very vocal during mating.

Incubation

You should record the weight and size of the eggs along with the date of nesting after the eggs have been collected. This will serve as an aid as when to expect the eggs to hatch. (Incubation times of individual

Dry Nest

Some tortoises will dig what many keepers call an exploratory nest or dry nest. This means the female digs and then abandons the nest without finishing it. It is not certain whether she gets interrupted and then abandons the site or whether she finds some indication that the original site is not a good place for the nest. The tortoise will not usually cover up the abandoned nest.

species will be listed in the species accounts in later chapters.)

Incubation Medium

The eggs should be placed into an incubation medium that will hold moisture and not get moldy. Good incubation media are sand, Perlite, vermiculite, and coconut husk, or you can use a mixture of those substances; they are all excellent incubation media. Tortoise eggs need a fairly humid environment, so the media should be moistened with water. Start with a ratio of 1:1 water to substrate by weight. It is better that the substrate be too dry than too moist. Too much moisture and the eggs will swell up and crack, but by providing too little moisture the eggs will dry out. The best indicator as to how much moisture is adequate is to ball up the moist substrate. It should be just moist enough to holds its form and not fall apart. This is a general starting point, because over time the keeper should get a feel of what the proper moisture content should be.

Egg Containers

Any plastic shoe box should serve well as a container in which to place the substrate and the eggs. It is up to the keeper whether to place holes in the container to allow for air circulation or not. If holes are not drilled into the container, open the lid on a regular basis, because the eggs do exchange gases and they do require fresh air.

A more recent means of incubating eggs is to place the egg into a plastic egg tray having holes drilled into the tray or on a grate to prevent the eggs from rolling around. This tray or grate is placed over standing water in a shoe box so that the eggs are not touching the water. The box should have a lid to cover the eggs. When using this method, the shoe box needs to be ventilated. The eggs are then placed into an incubator.

The Incubator

The incubator should be set up and tested long before any eggs are expected. Keepers should have an incubator that will maintain good stable temperatures. There are many incubators on

Other Nesting Habits

The Asian brown tortoise has a unique nesting behavior. Asian brown females actually scrape together leaf litter to build a nesting mound. They then deposit their eggs inside the mound. The decomposition of the leaf litter most likely also provides heat as the vegetation decomposes. The female then sits on the mound, where she guards it and tends to it for a while after nesting.

Another tortoise with a unique behavior pattern is the sulcata. A female sulcata digs a pre-nest that is as big as its body and as deep as the tortoise is tall. The female will then construct the actual nest for the eggs inside this pre-nest.

the market. Most are marketed for the poultry industry, but with the popularity of keeping reptiles on the rise many coming onto the market are designed for reptiles. The benefit of purchasing an incubator is that almost everything you need will be included in the package.

It is not very difficult to construct your own incubator by starting with insulated box (that you can construct yourself or purchase) or with a Styrofoam container, such as a cooler or a box used for shipping tropical fish. Some pet stores are willing to give these boxes away. Heating can be provided by a heat mat or ceramic heater. Temperature control is provided by a pulse thermostat or thermal wafer thermostat. The pulse thermostat is the more expensive option but offers the greatest accuracy. A separate temperature monitoring device should the used to crosscheck any automatic thermostat. Digital thermometers that record the highest and lowest temperatures within a 24-hour-period are particularly useful in that they allow you to see the entire range of temperatures that exist inside the incubator. Constructing your own incubator is recommended if you expect to produce a large amount of eggs, otherwise it is

Indoor nesting box for *Testudo* and similar species. The shredded newspaper provides cover and encourages the female to nest beneath it.

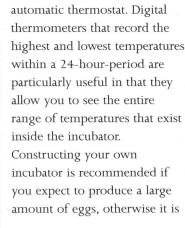

probably more cost efficient to purchase a commercially available incubator. The incubation temperature should be set to a range of 84° to 90°F (29° to 32°C) for most tortoises, depending on whether you want an equal mix of males and females or more of one sex than the other.

Leopard tortoise nesting. After nesting, the female will cover the nest to make it difficult to find.

Temperature-Dependent Sex Determination

It was mentioned earlier that the sex of developing tortoises is determined by the temperature at which the embryonic tortoises were incubated. This is called temperature-dependent sex determination (TSD). Tortoises do not have X or Y chromosomes, so it is not random chance that controls the determination of the sex. The sex of a hatching tortoise is determined by a specific temperature. A temperature below that specific temperature produces males and anything above that temperature produces females. That specific temperature is called the crossover temperature; it is 86°F (30°C) for most species of tortoises. This is the temperature at which a keeper can expect a 50/50 ratio of males to females among the hatchlings. The studies that are available report that the crossover temperature is quite exact, but there has to be some variance among individuals, because a breeder will sometimes get a hatchling that is the sex opposite the one that would be indicated by the incubation temperature.

The Tortoise Egg

The tortoise egg is a hard-shelled structure that is made up of tiny little plates. Under the shell is a leather-like

Female leopard tortoise with her clutch of eggs. Most breeders remove the eggs from the nest for artificial incubation.

membrane that contains the yolk and albumen. If the egg is fertile, it will also contain the embryo. The structure of the egg allows for the exchange of gases and fluids, which is important to note for a few reasons. When marking the egg it is recommended that a pencil be used because there is little to no chance of the marking matter getting into the egg because it is nonchemical, unlike ink. Chemical-based markers should not be used, because it is possible that the chemicals in the ink can cross the egg barrier with unknown results. It is believed that air moves in and out of the egg to replenish oxygen, which is why air circulation around the eggs should be provided by either making ventilation holes in the egg-holding container or occasionally opening the egg container and incubator to air out the eggs.

Along with the exchange of air there is an exchange of moisture, which is why the humidity around the egg is so important. If there is too much moisture the eggs will swell and crack. When this happens it usually happens slowly, so the keeper can reduce the umidity. If cracks do appear the inner membrane will usually keep the contents of the egg intact, and the keeper should not take any further action. Not enough humidity could cause the egg to dry out; detecting a lack of humidity can be performed by the process called "candling" the

Egg Binding

Occasionally some nesting behavior—pacing, digging—is observed, but the tortoise refuses to nest and lay eggs. In this situation, she should be watched closely. As long as she is acting normally and eating there should be no cause for concern, but if she suddenly slows down and stops eating, you need to take her to a veterinarian. X-rays should be taken to see whether she might be egg-bound. The technical term for egg binding is dystocia. This is a condition in which the tortoise cannot or will not deposit the eggs. The reasons for the condition are not always clear. Sometimes an egg is malformed and blocks the passage, and sometimes a female retains her eggs due to lack of a suitable nesting site.

Depending on what X-rays reveal, the vet may administer a drug (actually a hormone) called oxytocin. This will usually induce the tortoise to deposit the eggs, but oxytocin should be used only if totally necessary. If all else fails to get the tortoise to pass the eggs, they can be surgically removed; this procedure is hazardous, however, and should be used only as a last resort.

In Situ Incubation

Tortoise eggs do not have to be removed from the nest and artificially incubated, regardless of whether the eggs were deposited outdoors or in the indoor enclosure. In some cases they can be left to develop right in the nest. Whether or not this is possible depends on whether the eggs avoid freezing and whether the climate is similar to the climate of the tortoise's natural habitat (if the tortoise nest is located outdoors; if indoors the keeper must provide a suitable climate). While leaving the eggs where they were laid is possible, it's best not to do things that way—too many unknowns are involved. For example, there is a good chance that predators or insects can get to the eggs. Weather is also an unpredictable factor that can harm outdoor eggs through flooding, overheating, freezing, or drought. Indoor nests present fewer unknowns, but there is still less control than if the eggs are removed and incubated.

egg. Candling is done by holding a small pen or fiber optic light against the side of the egg to illuminate the contents of the egg. If the egg is losing moisture a circular cap or air pocket will show up when the egg is candled. The keeper can then add moisture to the substrate or place a small open container of water or moistened sponge into the egg container.

Development

The development of the eggs is based mainly on the temperature at which the egg is incubated. Temperature will determine the sex of the tortoise and also the rate at which the embryo develops. At higher temperatures the tortoise will develop sooner and at lower temperatures it will take longer. Some keepers might think they are going to get their hatchlings quicker by using very high temperatures. But temperatures that are too high cause deformities ranging from an abnormal number of scutes to missing eyes and worse. Genetics and natural development play a part in causing deformities, of course, but temperatures are the element the keeper can control to prevent this particular issue. A temperature range of 84° to 90°F (29° to 32°C) will not cause deformities. The time it takes for a tortoise to develop is going to vary from species to species and between individual clutches within a single species. Most of the tortoises in the genus *Testudo* hatch out in approximately 60 days, but the leopard tortoise can take as long as 400 days. This demonstrates how extreme the incubation time can be among the different tortoises.

When an egg is deposited it is normally a translucent white color. If the egg is fertile, it will start to chalk. The egg will develop either a cap or a band of chalk white and become less translucent. The caps can develop on the top or at either end of the egg. This will vary from species to species and among individuals but is consistent within a clutch. If and when an egg chalks the chalking will usually occur within a few days of the egg's being laid, with the exception of those species in which the eggs go through diapause (resting period; see section below).

If an egg is not fertile it will not chalk and remains a translucent color. When infertile eggs are candled they usually contain an air bubble that will move as the egg is moved. This is not the same as the condition caused when an egg becomes dehydrated. When an egg is dehydrated the air bubble is the membrane pulling away from the egg shell, and it will not move when the egg is moved.

The development of the egg can be seen by candling. The embryo develops at or near the top of the egg and first shows up as a small pink spot. The pink spot grows along with the veins to the yolk that feeds the embryo. Eventually the tortoise body gets larger and slowly blocks out any view of the inside of the egg, which is when candling is no longer effective.

Diapause

It is believed that some tortoise eggs require a rest period during which the egg does not develop. It is in a state that seems like suspended animation. This probably is an adaptation to hostile environmental conditions, such as winter or the dry season. Some eggs seem to need a drop in temperature for a time period to act as a type of activator to get the egg to start to develop. The flat-tailed tortoise is one species that seems to need a temperature drop. The temperature of the flat-tailed tortoise eggs is dropped to about 59°F

A hatching tortoise, such as this pancake tortoise, will pip its egg and then remain inside it for an additional day or so before fully emerging.

(15°C) when the eggs are laid. The temperature remains low for at least 30 days and then slowly is raised again. This treatment usually induces development. Some keepers have cooled the eggs back down for another cooling period if the eggs do not develop when the temperature is brought up. When the temperatures are returned to normal for a second time, the eggs often begins to develop. No one knows how many tortoises require a diapause, but it appears that many tortoises do. Many species that lay their eggs in the fall and have them hatch out in the spring, which is especially evident in *Testudo* species.

Hatching

When the tortoise gets ready to hatch it starts scratching the inside wall of the egg with either its egg tooth or its claws. The egg tooth is a pointy horn on the tip of the beak below the nostrils, which the tortoise uses to punch a hole in the shell. The egg tooth falls off shortly after hatching. The breaking of the inner membrane of the egg causes the egg to change color, going from a chalky white to a mottled white and darker grayish or bluish white. This varies from species to species, with some species going straight to punching a hole in the egg before any color change can be noticed in the egg. With those eggs that do change color you can expect to see the tortoise pip (the act of punching a hole in the egg with the egg tooth) within a day or two of the color change. Most tortoises that have just pipped them will remain in the egg until they absorb all the yolk. This can take up to three or four days, at which time the tortoise will break out of the egg entirely.

Occasionally a tortoise will hatch out before all the yolk has been absorbed. In this case the keeper should remove any remaining egg shell and place the tortoise (on top of the remaining yolk sac) inside a small container to keep the tortoise relatively immobile. Before putting the tortoise inside the container, line the container with moist gauze or cloth to keep the yolk sac moist and the tortoise humid. Don't try to cover the yolk with anything, because that usually induces the tortoise to try to claw the restraint off, which will lead to the rupturing of the yolk sac. Once the yolk sac is ruptured it is very likely the tortoise will develop a septic infection, a condition that is nearly impossible to treat in a neonate tortoise and from which the tortoise will not survive.

Some suggestions for a suitable container into which to place a neonate with an external yolk sac would be a teacup or coffee mug—sufficient in size for all but the largest species. The yolk sac should be absorbed in two or three days, but this will depend on the size of the yolk sac that remains.

When a tortoise hatches out it is usually going to be folded or deformed by the shape of the egg regardless of whether it hatches out with or without the yolk sac. The tortoise should be placed on a hard flat surface covered with a moist paper towel or cloth. A plastic shoebox without the incubation medium should be good for this. The box can remain in the incubator until the shell has assumed its natural form in a few days; when this occurs the hatchling can be moved into its enclosure. At this time the keeper will have a complete and well-formed hatchling that can go on and breed when its time comes.

Providing For Hatchling Tortoises

It is important to have the provisions for the hatchlings in place before they actually hatch. This will prevent a great deal of worry because when the eggs hatch it is similar to going

Hatching leopard tortoises. In this species, the eggs may take up to 400 days to hatch.

This leopard tortoise has hatched before absorbing all its yolk. When this happens, the keeper needs to provide the baby a few days of special care.

out and obtaining a new group of tortoises. An important point to consider is that you will need to maintain these new tortoises until you can find new homes for them. It is likely you will be able to sell, trade, or give them to other keepers, but you should be prepared to house and care for your hatchlings for as long as it takes to place them in appropriate homes.

Plastic sweater boxes are perfect nurseries for smaller tortoises, and larger species will need somewhat larger accommodations. These are simple to set up and easy to obtain. The container can be used with or without the lid. Be sure to place air holes in the sides and the lid if the lid is used. The lid can be useful to keep out any harmful pests or keep in moisture. However, do not to let it get too moist. Always provide a dry section in a hatchling container.

Variations and Oddities

Tortoise keepers are breeding tortoises more frequently and in larger quantities than ever before. The odds of producing strange genetic variations increases as more and more tortoises are produced. Sometimes these variations are considered desirable, such as albino tortoises. Relatively many albino and oddly colored tortoises of numerous species are being produced, and they can be attractive. The keeper should remember that our captive tortoises are pets, and there is nothing inherently wrong with albino pets even though they would be unlikely to survive in nature.

The Strong Survive

I don't recommend helping a tortoise that has trouble hatching to emerge from the egg. Not all hatchlings are fit to survive, so it is usually best to allow the tortoise to fend for itself. If it has the strength to hatch out on its own, it has a very good chance of surviving. Tortoises that don't make it out of the egg on their own are often unhealthy in some way and are unlikely to survive.

Another oddity that presents itself on occasion is the two-headed tortoise. Two-headedness is not a genetic trait, but it does occur on a relatively frequent basis. Most two-headed tortoises don't survive, but quite a few survived for many years. This aspect only adds one more interesting dimension to the world of tortoise keeping.

Final Thoughts on Tortoise Breeding

It would seem that a person could actually make a living out of raising tortoises. There are many keepers who have turned tortoise keeping into a business, but the expenditure of time and money, in addition to the effort of caring for and keeping tortoises, is immense. It is not a good idea to pursue this hobby with the intention of making a profit. For each successful (that is, profitable) tortoise breeder there are many who failed. A huge amount of luck and work goes into this endeavor, and even then there are no guarantees of success. If you decide to breed your tortoises, do it for the experience and not for the profit.

Some odd color variations (called morphs) are highly desired by breeders and fetch high prices, such as the ivory morph of the sulcata.

Testudo hermanni

Chapter 5

Health Care

Health care is an area of tortoise care that keepers frequently do not properly consider before deciding to keep a tortoise or tortoises. It is important to make provisions for when a tortoise is going to require veterinary care because that is not a question of *whether* something is going to go wrong but rather one of *when* something is going to go wrong. A cold snap could leave your leopard tortoise with a respiratory infection, or birds bathing in the water bowl could transmit intestinal parasites to your turtles. The wise keeper is ready to deal with these unforeseen problems.

I recommend that a part of the household budget be set aside for veterinary bills that are sure to come up at some point. Too many tortoise keepers cannot take their tortoises to the veterinarian because they lack of money. They often wait until it is too late to do anything for the unfortunate animals. There really is no reason for a tortoise to suffer for its keeper's improper planning.

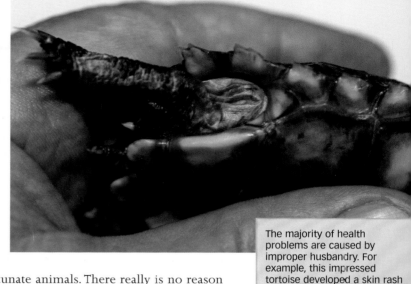

The majority of health problems are caused by improper husbandry. For example, this impressed tortoise developed a skin rash from being kept too moist.

Husbandry and Health

The best course of action to reduce the chances of needing a veterinary visit is through preventive maintenance. Excellent day-to-day care of a tortoise goes a long way toward preventing health problems. Heat and hydration have been stressed throughout this guide because these are two of the factors that have the greatest influence on so many health issues that occur with tortoises in captivity. If you have those two elements in balance the chances of needing veterinary care are drastically reduced, provided you've obtained a healthy tortoise to begin with. Diet also will play a major role in the health of the tortoise, but not as much as heat and hydration.

When a tortoise is dehydrated, all its bodily functions are affected. If the dehydration is severe enough, organ failure occurs. Humidity can be a benefit to the tortoise, but it can also harm the tortoise that does not have the option to dry out on occasion. Even the moisture-loving tortoises such as the forest hingebacks and the Asian brown tortoise need to be provided with the opportunity to dry out or they can develop mold or fungus on the skin.

Reptile Veterinarians

Should a tortoise become ill, it has the best chance of recovering if treated by a veterinarian who has experience with—or better yet, specializes in—reptile medicine. They are commonly listed as exotic veterinarians because their practice treats exotic animals, such as birds, amphibians, and reptiles. Even among the exotic-pet vets, it's best to further refine your search to ones who specialize in reptiles or at least treat them frequently. Those vets will have the equipment and knowledge base best suited to helping your turtle.

Finding a local reptile veterinarian can be difficult, but it has gotten easier recently. The greater number of people keeping reptile pets has given rise to a greater number of veterinarians who treat them. The Internet has become an invaluable resource for finding a good reptile veterinarian. Many groups on the Web have compiled local lists for veterinarians who have been recommended by other tortoise keepers. The website of the Association of Reptilian and Amphibian Veterinarians, www.arav.org, also has a list of qualified herp veterinarians. Once you find a vet who treats reptiles, record all the contact information in an easily accessible place. Call and find out what the hours of operation are and how the vet handles emergencies. Some vets will see an emergency themselves, while others refer to specialty emergency clinics. It the latter is the case, follow up with the emergency clinic and make sure they take tortoises.

Special provisions are needed by keepers of the larger tortoises, such as the sulcata or the Aldabra tortoise. If one of those tortoises needs a veterinarian visit, special arrangements are going to be needed. Many veterinarians will make house calls, but they can be quite expensive. The other option is to be prepared to move a 200-plus-pound tortoise, which is no simple task without the proper equipment.

Quarantine

Anytime a new tortoise is added to a group there is going to be a risk of it bringing some kind of disease into the established group. That risk varies depending on the source of the tortoise; there is less risk when the new tortoise is captive-bred than if it is wild-caught or farm-raised. (It is best to consider farm-raised tortoises to be the same as wild-caught ones because they are raised in a free-range setup in the

Tortoise Insurance

Within recent years some insurance companies have started to offer pet health insurance. If a keeper has more than one tortoise or has multiple pets, this insurance may be worth the cost, because with the increased number of pets there is going to be an increase in the need for veterinary care. Veterinary visits can be quite costly, so a veterinary financial war chest is always a good idea. While not all veterinarians accept this insurance, the number that do is increasing all the time.

natural habitat and are exposed to many of the same parasites, bacteria, etc., as wild tortoises would be.) When adding a tortoise to an already existing group there is a preventive measure that many tortoise keepers use to reduce the chances of introducing disease into the existing group. This measure is quarantining the new animal for a period of time away from the group. The ideal quarantine would

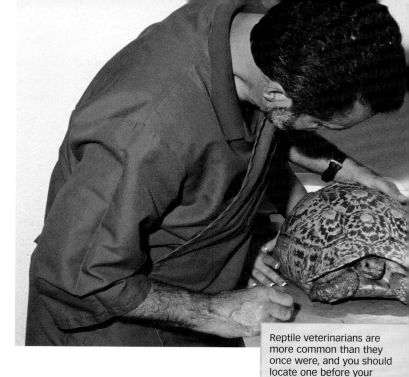

Reptile veterinarians are more common than they once were, and you should locate one before your tortoise has an emergency.

be to have the new tortoise in a totally separate building from the existing group, but this is not always practical for the average tortoise keeper. The next best thing would be to house the tortoise in an area separated from the main group, which most tortoise keepers can do. The idea is not to allow the new tortoise to come in contact with the existing group.

To avoid contaminating the existing group, the best practice is to perform all of the daily care and feeding duties for the existing group first and then do so for the quarantined turtle. Keep all of the equipment and furnishings used for in the quarantined tortoise from contacting those used for the main group. Wash your hands whenever you are moving between groups; if you need to step into the enclosures you may want to have a pair of old shoes that only go into the quarantine enclosure.

Quarantine Duration

It's up to you to determine how long the quarantine period should be, but a minimum of one month is suggested. Most tortoise keepers will recommend a period of six months, even though any major maladies that are going to reveal themselves are going to do so in the first month. A longer period is always going to be better for observation purposes. There are maladies—including some protozoans and viruses—that may remain hidden for years, so extending the length of quarantine past one month is not a guarantee that the new tortoise is completely healthy.

Quarantine Setup

The quarantine setup should provide the same conditions as the housing for the main group to allow the quarantined turtle to acclimate to those conditions. Keep the enclosure simple by including an easily cleaned hiding place or box but not much else in the way of furnishings. Place a water dish in one corner or against a wall so the tortoise can find it easily. It is suggested to use carpeting, cloth, or plain newsprint as a floor covering so fecal samples can be easily observed and collected for veterinary examination. Humidity and temperature should be appropriate for the species.

Assessing Health During Quarantine

While the tortoise is in quarantine, observe it carefully for any abnormal behavior—not feeding, not drinking, remaining in one place. Those are the main indicators that something is not correct. Do give the new animal time to acclimate before becoming overly concerned; a few days of not eating is likely just a reaction to the strange surroundings.

Tongue Color and Health A prime indication of the health of a tortoise is its tongue color. A tortoise's tongue should be a light pink color, not yellow or white. An abnormally colored tongue can indicate anemia, which is a sign of infection.

The easiest way to check the tongue color of a new tortoise is to watch the tortoise when it is eating and look at the tongue when it goes to take a bite. If the tortoise is not eating the keeper can gently pull and hold one of the forelegs back to access the head while carefully using a toothpick to gently open the mouth. Start at the back corner of the mouth and

Hold the Ivermectin

Ivermectin is a commonly prescribed antiparastic drug. It is used in dogs, cats, horses, and some other animals. However, this medicine is highly toxic to tortoises and other turtles. Never use ivermectin for treating parasites in tortoises, and if you need to use it to treat other pets, keep it far away from your turtles.

gently push the toothpick inside. The tortoise will usually try to dispel the toothpick by opening the mouth, allowing the keeper to carefully get the toothpick further into the mouth, thus holding the jaws open and making the tongue visible.

This method can also be used to administer medication should need arise. As the tortoise becomes acclimated, you should occasionally handle the tortoise's head to gain its trust, which makes the task of opening the mouth easier. Eventually the tortoise will allow the keeper to hold the head between the thumb and the forefinger while the keeper gently pulls down on the lower jaw to open the mouth. This technique requires time, patience, and practice but is well worth the effort for future inspections and possible medication administration. The inspection of the tongue color is an important part of the initial assessment during the quarantine period.

Veterinary Care During the quarantine period, ideally the keeper will take the new tortoise to the veterinarian for a thorough exam. This should include a physical exam, a fecal exam, and complete blood testing. The exam not only will screen out blood-borne parasites and disease but also will give a good assessment of kidney and liver function. The veterinarian may suggest other tests depending on the tortoise and what the first tests reveal.

At a minimum, it is recommended that the feces be taken to a veterinarian for a fecal exam. This will determine whether there are any obvious internal parasites present. If you cannot take the fecal sample to the vet immediately, it should be refrigerated (in a well-sealed container) but not frozen. If parasites are present, the vet will prescribe appropriate medication.

A healthy tortoise's tongue is light pink in color, not yellow or white.

Signs of Health Problms

Although it is impossible to diagnose most tortoise health problems by just looking at the tortoise, there are warning signs the keeper can be on the lookout for with nothing but a visual inspection. The most basic sign has already been mentioned, and that is when the tortoise starts slowing down and refusing food and water. This can also occur if humidity and temperature are inappropriate, so check those first before assuming the issue is a parasite or infection.

Another early warning sign is the tortoise's passing loose, watery stools. While this subject is not one of the most pleasant topics of discussion, it is one that is quite important and frequently comes up among tortoise keepers. Normal feces should be firm and well-formed pellets. If the feces are watery, first consider the diet because items with a high water content, such as melons and iceberg lettuce, will also cause watery feces. Abnormal feces are one the most common signs of internal parasites.

Another sign to look for is nasal discharge or any kind of wheezing that can be heard as the tortoise breathes. This in itself is not always a sign of ill health, especially after the tortoise has had a drink of water. In conjunction with other signs, nasal discharge and/or wheezing are a cause for concern. Gently poking the tortoise in the nose will usually cause the tortoise to withdraw quickly and expel air just as quickly. If there is any wheezing to be heard it will present itself then.

The eyes can be good indicators of stress and ill health. If the eyes are held shut or tearing up, suspect a problem. In extreme cases the eyes will become sunken, which is a sign of dehydration. When tortoises are physically stressed by a parasite overload or bacterial infection, they will sometimes refuse water even if they are soaked. Sunken eyes usually follow along with a loss of weight.

The forelimbs should not have a hooked appearance or appear flat in cross section. They should be plump and round. Some of the tortoises, such as the hingebacks, naturally have hooked and flat forelimbs, but a similar appearance becomes extremely exaggerated in health-

Preventive Medicine

Farm-raised and wild-caught tortoises should be treated for protozoans and worms for at least three weeks during quarantine. The most common drugs used for this purpose are metronidazole for the protozoans and fenbendazole for the worms. This treatment has been shown to increase the rate of successful survival and acclimation of these tortoises. Consult a veterinarian to obtain the medications and determine the exact dosages the tortoise needs.

stressed animals.

If your tortoise displays any of the mentioned signs—and especially if it displays several of them—take it to a vet for assessment. The sooner you do so, the better chance your turtle will have for recovery.

Parasites

Parasites are one of the most common problems seen in tortoises. They are most common in wild-caught and farm-raised tortoises, but they occasionally show up in captive-bred ones. There are two major types of parasites: external parasites, called ectoparasites, and internal parasites, called endoparasites. Ectoparasites are found on the shell or skin, while endoparasites can be found anywhere inside the tortoise. The most common endoparasites are found in the gut, but they can infest the blood, liver, lungs, and other areas.

The sunken, half-closed eyes of this Greek tortoise are signs that it is seriously ill.

External Parasites

Ectoparasites are commonly found in the folds of skin or pockets of the shell where the skin is exposed. Two common external parasites of tortoises are ticks and botflies. Mites, parasites that commonly infest lizards and snakes, only rarely affect tortoises.

Botflies

There are more than one hundred species of botflies and the larvae are parasitic. They can be devastating to a tortoise collection. Blowflies and flesh flies are similarly parasitic—the use of the term *botfly* in this discussion includes all the parasitic flies. The fly will lay eggs either on the skin or inside an open wound. When the eggs hatch, the larvae burrow into the host and feed on the tissues. This happens mostly with debilitated tortoises, along with tortoises kept in filthy and damp conditions. The botfly is rarely a problem for tortoises that are healthy and kept in good clean conditions. Special attention should be given to forest tortoises because of their moist keeping conditions. Tortoises kept indoors under proper conditions are very unlikely to encounter botflies. If possible, move an injured tortoise indoors or to a screened-in enclosure to prevent botflies from laying eggs in the wound.

If botfly infestation does become a problem, it can be dealt with if caught early and the tortoise is taken to the veterinarian. If it is not caught early enough, the outcome for the tortoise is usually not very good. Each time a tortoise is picked up the keeper should inspect it closely by looking over all the exposed skin. Pay particular attention to the areas under the tail along with those areas behind the retracted legs and head. With the more shy tortoises it is suggested to gently handle the tortoises to try and break them of their shyness.

The sign of a botfly infestation (also called flystrike and myiasis) is a small lump or swelling under the skin. Frequently there will be a small hole in this lump. This lump is filled with fly larvae. A veterinarian will slice open the lump, remove the larvae, and stitch the wound closed. Antibiotics are often prescribed to prevent the site from becoming infected.

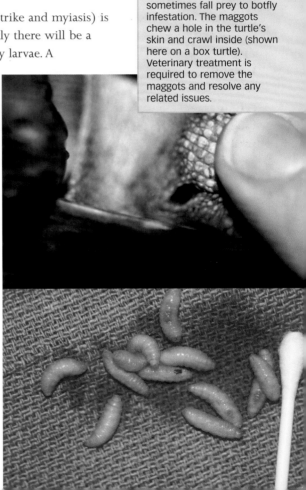

Tortoises kept outdoors sometimes fall prey to botfly infestation. The maggots chew a hole in the turtle's skin and crawl inside (shown here on a box turtle). Veterinary treatment is required to remove the maggots and resolve any related issues.

Ticks Most people are somewhat familiar with ticks. These arachnids attach to a host's skin and use their sucking mouthparts to feed on the blood. Typical areas where ticks are found are where the skin attaches to the shell and in the folds of skin at the base of the neck and the limbs. The keeper should pay particular attention to moving the limbs and tail when examining for ticks. On the shell, the parasites can be found wherever there is exposed skin between the scutes and can also be found where the shell has been damaged and subsequently healed.

Tortoises in the wild can carry some ticks without much problem because some are

Gopher tortoise with a tick attached to it (circled). Ticks are common on wild tortoises.

knocked off or abandon the tortoise as it forages through the underbrush. In captivity they can become a problem because ticks are forced to keep feeding over and over again on the same tortoises. Additionally, if the tick reproduces all of the young ticks will then feed on the tortoises as well. Ticks debilitate their hosts as they feed.

Another problem with ticks is that they are vectors for transmitting blood-borne diseases. If a new tortoise is carrying ticks and the tortoise is introduced to a group of established tortoises, the ectoparasites could then transfer over to these tortoises. The established tortoises could then become infected with any blood-borne infection that might be carried by the new tortoise. There is a chance the established tortoises might not tolerate the infection as well as the new tortoise. All of the tortoises would need to be treated for the ticks as well as the infection—assuming the infection doesn't just kill them.

The greatest chance of introducing ectoparasites comes from adding a wild-caught or farm-raised tortoise to a group. Any new tortoise should be thoroughly and carefully inspected for ticks and other parasites before it is housed with the established group. This is another reason quarantine is such a good idea.

Ticks can be manually removed by firmly grasping the tick with tweezers as close to the tortoise's skin as possible. Pull the tick straight out with a steady motion—do not twist it. Effort should be made to get the whole tick out including its head, which will be under the skin. If the head detaches and cannot easily be removed, leave it in the skin and monitor the area closely for any signs of infection. After removing a tick, clean the area and wash your hands. To help prevent infection, dab a little antibiotic ointment onto the site where the tick was attached.

Internal Parasites

The chances of introducing endoparasites to an existing group are greatest when a new tortoise is added. Captive-bred tortoises present the least likely chance of carrying endoparasites. If the breeder of the new tortoise maintains good hygiene conditions, the risk of contamination by endoparasites from a captive-raised tortoise is virtually eliminated.

An important point to remember is that a tortoise can tolerate a certain level of parasite infestation before it shows any outward signs of invasion. It is neither necessary nor even possible to eliminate every single parasite a tortoise may have. Many veterinarians now consider having a small population of parasites to be normal. The key is the health of the tortoise. If the tortoise is otherwise healthy, a small population of parasites should not alarm the keeper.

Parasites often present a problem to the tortoise when it becomes stressed. Long-term stress impairs the immune system, so when a tortoise becomes stressed any parasites it may have multiply unchecked by the tortoise's own defenses. Stress can be caused by any number of issues, including inadequate diet, inappropriate temperatures, breeding, and

Unsightly Mites

There are some mites occasionally found in tortoise enclosures, but they usually are not parasitic. These little white mites occur where there is an overly moist substrate in an enclosure that is allowed to remain warm and stagnant for a long period of time. The mites will congregate in the substrate and under any furniture, such as water bowls and rocks. These particular mites are more of an aesthetic nuisance than anything else and do not pose a threat to the tortoise. These mites are easily removed by cleaning the enclosure and the associated furniture.

overcrowding. When a tortoise is sold by a breeder, the new environment may cause stress. New tortoise keepers often have issues with parasites because their inexperience causes some aspect of care to be inadequate.

Tortoises maintained outdoors have access to plenty of roughage, a good diet, and sunshine, which helps put them in ideal health to tolerate any small parasite load. These tortoises are going to encounter parasites from the ground from bird droppings and inside any snails or insects they may happen to consume. In a healthy tortoise, there is a balance between the parasite and the host that does not impair the tortoise's health.

Diagnosing Parasites It is difficult to diagnose an infection caused by endoparasites (or bacteria) by external observation; the outward signs can be subtle, and different pathogens can cause the same symptoms. The only way to properly diagnose an endoparasite is through microscopic examination. The easiest of these microscopic examinations is by conducting a fecal examination or a cloacal swab from the tortoise. The cloacal swab is not as accurate as the fecal exam but is useful when a vet cannot get a fecal sample. Another method to obtain an internal sample is the stomach wash, in which a veterinarian flushes the stomach with a saline solution and examines the fluid under a microscope. Lastly, a vet can check for internal parasites with a surgical biopsy. Endoscopic surgery has made this minimally invasive. Tissue samples are usually taken from multiple organs and examined under a microscope with the aid of various

Both wild-caught and farm-raised tortoises frequently carry parasites, so it a good idea to take one to the veterinarian soon after acquiring it.

stains. This last method is the best diagnostic tool for *Entamoeba* infections.

Types of Internal Parasites

Internal parasites can be broken down into two major groups: single-celled protozoans and multicelled helminths. Helminths are worms; parasitic helminths can come from the following worm groups: nematodes (roundworms), trematodes (flukes), and cestodes (tapeworms).

Protozoans seem to present the greatest challenge to tortoise keepers, with flagellates and amoebas being the most problematic of this group. These two internal parasites are easily transmitted between turtles. An additional issue posed by them is that they sometimes have a dormant life stage called a cyst. The cyst stage is imbedded in the tortoise's tissues and may not be shed in the feces, so it is difficult to detect. The common drugs that are use to eradicate these parasites normally kill only the adult stage and do not harm the cysts. It is for this reason that when treating for protozoans it is important to find a medication that will address all the stages or use a medication for a long-enough period to allow the intermediate stages to develop into adults and be eliminated.

Fun With Microscopes

It is a good idea for a tortoise keeper to obtain a microscope and learn how to use it. A used microscope will be fairly inexpensive. There are many informative and inexpensive books about reptile parasites that will explain slide preparation and parasite identification. Most of the larger parasites and bacteria are easily seen and identified in a simple float. A float is a prepared by breaking up a tortoise fecal sample in saline and putting a drop of this solution on a slide. This is not only fun and fascinating but it could alert the keeper that a veterinarian visit is in order.

Most protozoans can be eliminated with the use of Metronidazole. It is a very safe drug to use in tortoises but has been implicated in causing joint problems in birds when administered in high doses. When used as directed as a vet, there should be no concern for the tortoise keeper with Metronidazole.

Helminths can have dramatic negative effects on health if the tortoise is stressed or contracts an unrelated health condition. The only way most of the parasitic worms are detected and diagnosed is if the tortoise passes the worms, part of the worms, and/or the eggs in its droppings. Depending on the organism, the worms may be visible or the evidence may be microscopic. If there is evidence of helminths, the tortoise should receive veterinary care.

The nematode worms include lungworms, threadworms, hookworms, and pinworms. These parasites are relatively common in many of the species of *Testudo* when they are maintained outdoors. Pinworms are the most frequently encountered by tortoise keepers because they are commonly found in most lawns. Tortoises kept outdoors will pick up pinworms as they graze, especially if the soil is constantly moist. Normally the pinworm population inside a healthy tortoise is kept in check by the roughage in the diet. If the population grows out of control the pinworms will be easily detected in the feces, appearing as tiny white to translucent worms. If the pinworms are readily visible in the droppings the tortoise should be treated, but otherwise a small population of pinworms causes no harm. Recently some keepers have come to believe that pinworms may actually serve a function within the digestive tract of the tortoise.

The trematodes, the flukes, do not occur in tortoises very often and are usually seen only in wild-caught tortoises. They crop up occasionally in tortoises kept in moist conditions, such as the forest hingebacks and Asian brown tortoise. The trematodes that are the easiest to detect are those that are found inside the mouth. They are easily seen as tiny black dashes against the light color of the inside of the mouth. Flukes can also occur throughout the digestive systems. Flukes always require veterinary treatment.

Cestodes are the tapeworms, and they make their home within the digestive tract attached to the lining of the intestines. They can be very large, so their feeding can have a drastic impact on the tortoise if it is not eating properly. This is another helminth that is not commonly found in tortoises besides wild-caught ones.

Infectious Diseases

Bacteria and viruses occur in tortoises with the about same frequency as parasites. As with the parasites, captive-bred tortoises are less likely to carry bacteria and viruses than farm-raised and wild-caught ones. In some cases, tortoises can harbor these pathogens for many years without any outward signs. Then, when the tortoise becomes stressed, the hidden

Wicked Worms

Some nematodes passed by tortoises can be amazingly large. In the past when wild-caught Egyptian tortoises were being imported, it was not uncommon for these little tortoises, which measure about 4 inches (10 cm) SCL, to pass a 4-inch (10-cm) roundworm! If a tortoise does pass such a parasite, it should be treated by a veterinarian to eradicate any nematodes that remain.

Flukes are uncommon parasites, although they are sometimes seen in the forest species, such as the Asian brown tortoise.

bacterium or virus will manifest and create a health issue. Many of the general signs of ill health can be caused by bacteria and viruses.

It can be very time consuming and costly to determine which bacteria is causing the infection and which antibiotic will be most effective against it. For this reason, most veterinarians will choose to use a broad-spectrum antibiotic, forgoing full diagnostic testing. If the broad-spectrum antibiotic is ineffective, the vet will do more complete testing. In many instances, the health of the tortoise is so stressed that there is not enough time for full diagnostics, making the administration of a broad-spectrum antibiotic the best option.

General Treatment

If there is evidence of a bacterial infection the first thing to do is to place the tortoise in an enclosure that holds a constant temperature between 80° and 90°F (27° and 32°C). This has the same effect as a fever: it boosts the immune system while inhibiting the bacteria. The tortoise should be soaked daily to make sure it is well hydrated. If the tortoise is eating, it may not require veterinary care. The tortoise's own immune system combined with the added heat and hydration may fend off the illness. Monitor its health closely. If its condition doesn't improve in a few days or if the signs of ill health get worse, quick veterinary care is needed.

Respiratory Infections

A runny nose can be a sign of a bacterial infection of the respiratory tract. It also can be a sign that there is a parasitic infestation, because the stress caused by the parasites has weakened the tortoise's immune system and allowed an infection to take hold. Other signs of respiratory infections include wheezing, a bubbling noise when breathing, and labored breathing. Labored breathing can be hard to notice in tortoises—if your turtle is pumping its head and legs as it breathes, it is having trouble breathing.

Russian tortoises are very susceptible to respiratory infections when they are kept too cold and too damp. Other species, notably leopard tortoises and forest hingebacks, often get respiratory infections when the keeping temperatures are too low.

If the discharge from the nostrils is watery and thin, the most likely issue is runny nose syndrome (RNS), frequently caused by bacteria in the genus *Mycoplasma*. These are very difficult to treat, and it is recommended that a veterinarian culture the bacteria to find a suitable antibiotic. It is currently thought that *Mycoplasma* often cannot be totally eradicated and instead must be suppressed until the tortoise is healthy enough for its immune system to keep the bacteria under control.

Septicemia

Bacteria are also usually responsible for blood infections, called septic infections or septicemia. These infections are seen most often in tortoises that are less than a year old. When septicemia gets to the extreme stage, blood

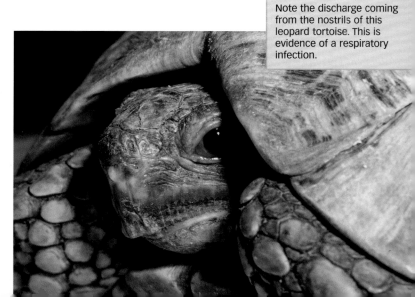

Note the discharge coming from the nostrils of this leopard tortoise. This is evidence of a respiratory infection.

Tortoises showing blood under the scutes of the shell are critically ill with septicemia.

will leak under the scutes of the shell. The blood then progresses throughout the layer between the scute and the bone of the shell to eventually seep out between the margins of the scutes. By the time the infection reaches this stage, the prognosis for the tortoise is dire, but treatment with antibiotics is sometimes successful. Also, the keeper should have noticed other signs of illness long before blood starts leaking into the shell. The earlier septicemia is caught, the better the chances that it can be cured. The underlying cause of a septic infection is usually kidney and/or liver failure brought on by parasites, dehydration, improper diet, or infections.

Herpes Virus

There are not many studies on the viruses of tortoises except for one virus, commonly referred to as a herpes virus. There is no cure for the virus; it is usually fatal, but there are some new drugs that can control or suppress the virus if it is caught early enough.

The virus is commonly spread from wild-caught tortoises but has been reported to be found in European-farmed tortoises, too (although this has not been confirmed at this time). The herpes virus can lie dormant for at least 10 years—based on the experiences of some tortoise keepers—and can be triggered by the simplest stressor. The virus is spread by direct contact from tortoise to tortoise. Tortoises use their sense of smell as a primary identifier, so when two tortoises meet it is not uncommon for the two to touch noses. This is the likeliest route of transmission. The virus is very unstable outside the host, which makes any transmission besides tortoise-to-tortoise unlikely.

Hygiene

All tortoise keepers should get into the habit of washing their hands with warm water and a good antibacterial soap after handling any tortoise. This washing regimen is especially important when handling tortoises from different enclosures. Tortoises are carriers of *Salmonella* bacteria, gram- negative bacteria that can settle in the digestive system of a person, where they release toxins that can cause a severe illness called salmonellosis. These bacteria are responsible for the enactment of the law that prohibits the sale of a tortoise under 4 inches (10 cm) SCL. The policy of good hygienic practices protects not only the tortoises but also the keeper and those people around the keeper.

The virus can be transmitted only when it is active, so a tortoise that shows any signs of the herpes virus should immediately be isolated. A runny nose is one of the first signs of that the virus has become active, with the nasal discharge being watery s in nature. This discharge is usually followed by the accumulation of a cheesy material in the mouth. This will eventually cover the entire mouth of the tortoise including the tongue.

A keeper can have a tortoise tested for herpes. A positive result does indicate the presence of the virus, but a negative result does not necessarily mean the virus is not present. When the virus is inactive, it often does not produce a positive test result.

Injuries

Despite a keeper's best efforts, there is always the chance for a tortoise to get injured. This can be the result of breeding aggression or the tortoise's falling from a tall rock platform in its enclosure or any number of other circumstances. For more minor injuries, the wound should first be cleaned with warm water followed by disinfection with povidone iodine or peroxide. When disinfecting, pat the area gently instead of wiping it because patting will cause less pain and has less risk of causing further damage to the area. Afterwards, it is a good idea to cover the wound with any topical antibiotic ointment to prevent a bacterial infection. The tortoise should be kept in a sterile and warm environment until the wound scabs. At that time it can be returned to its enclosure. If it is housed with other tortoises in the same enclosure, keep the tortoise separated until the wound is completely healed. For more serious wounds, such as a cracked shell caused by a serious fall or an attack by an animal resulting in severe trauma, a veterinarian should be consulted immediately.

Metabolic Bone Disease

Good environmental conditions promote proper digestion and metabolism in pet tortoises, but they cannot make up for an inadequate diet. A well-balanced and highly varied diet will assure raising a tortoise that has a form to be proud of. However, this does not always happen, and lack of success is usually caused by an oversight on the part of the keeper. You could be feeding too many plants that are high in oxalates or glucosinolates or may not be providing enough calcium (see Chapter 3). Caution should always be exercised you use foods containing these two chemical compounds, but the one nutritional element that presents more problems than the two mentioned is calcium.

Calcium deficiency usually results in metabolic bone disease (MBD). Although this disease has been declining in frequency among pet tortoises, it still occurs more often than it should. It is the most common nutritional illness of pet tortoises. One reason for this is that turtles have a lot of bone mass in the shell. The shell has evolved from the ribs; it has become modified into a protective covering. The calcium requirement to maintain this shell is immense. The shell serves not only as protection for a turtle but also as a calcium reserve that can mobilize calcium into the bloodstream when it is needed for any physiological processes.

Signs of MBD

The cheesy accumulation in the mouth of this Greek tortoise is due to a herpes infection.

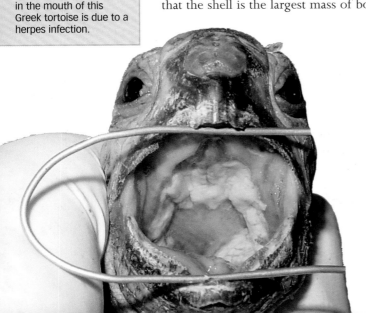

Tortoises with MBD will show various skeletal abnormalities. Given that the shell is the largest mass of bone in the body, MBD often shows up first in the shell. The shell may become soft or deformed. The jaws also become deformed fairly early in the progression of this disease. If allowed to progress further, jaw and shell deformities worsen, other bones become deformed, movement is impaired due to misshapen and easily fractured limbs, feeding may be impaired because of jaw deformities, and muscle tremors and generalized shaking occur.

Prevention and Treatment

Metabolic bone disease is easily preventable by feeding tortoises a varied diet, providing supplemental calcium, and giving them access to UVB. If MBD is suspected, a vet visit is in order. A veterinarian can determine whether MBD is indeed the issues through x-rays and blood testing. If the tortoise has MBD and is still in the earliest stages, the veterinarian may suggest adjustments to the care you are providing, such as providing more UVB lighting or adding more calcium supplements to the diet. More severe cases may require calcium injections or other treatment. If caught early, the problems created by MBD are usually reversible. Female tortoises that have had MBD seem to be more prone to egg binding.

Overgrown Beak and Nails

Tortoises that are kept indoors face some unique physical conditions that tortoises maintained outdoors do not. One important condition is the lack of sufficient hard surfaces to wear down the toenails and beak which can lead them to become overgrown, l eventually impairing or otherwise injuring the tortoise. Sometimes this will require manual trimming by the keeper.

The toenails can be clipped using any pet toenail clipper or emery board. Most tortoise toenails are translucent, so the veins are easily seen. Keep the trim below the veins to avoid causing pain and bleeding. If the vein is clipped a septic pencil can be used to stop the bleeding.

Using an emery board regularly on the tortoise's nails is a good form of preventive maintenance that can eliminate the need for trimming. It will also suffice for the beak. If the beak should require trimming, use an emery board or rotary grinding tool. Do not use any form of clipper or

Bell's hingeback with a mostly healed animal bite in its shell (circled). Animal bites in tortoises usually require emergency treatment.

Tortoise with an overgrown beak. If not treated, this condition will eventually prevent the turtle from eating.

scissors. Most tortoises will allow filing without having the keeper holding or restraining it if the keeper is gentle and gains the tortoise's confidence. The beak is trimmed by removing material parallel to the edge of the beak. The beak grows by having very thin layers laid down from the bone of the jaw outward. It is these fine layers that are being removed when the beak is being trimmed. If the keeper is not comfortable in attempting this, a veterinary visit is the next best option. Trimming can be reduced or eliminated by providing abrasive foods such as grass or hay along with offering food on a flat rock to help wear down the beak. Provide rocks and abrasive climbing surfaces to keep the nails in shape.

Conclusion

This section on health care covers the most important points for the average keeper and is intended to be just a foundation on subject. You should continue to do more of your own research on tortoise to add to this base.

Geochelone sulcata

Chapter 6

Desert Species

Quite a few tortoise species naturally occur in desert and other arid habitats. They are adapted to dry conditions with hot days and cool nights. The sampling of these species discussed here are among those most commonly kept by hobbyists, including the sulcata and Russian tortoises.

Other Desert Species

There are few other species besides those discussed in this chapter that can be kept in a similar fashion as the desert species. These include the desert tortoise (*Gopherus agassizii*) of the United States and northern Mexico and the bolson tortoise (*Gopherus flavomarginatus*) of Mexico. The latter species is unavailable in the hobby at this time. The Egyptian tortoise (*Testudo kleinmanni*) is a very small desert-dwelling tortoise from North Africa and the Middle East. It is rare in the hobby, but some breeders produce and sell this interesting little tortoise.

Egyptian tortoise

North African Greek Tortoise (*Testudo graeca*)

The information in this section will apply, with little adjustment, to all of the North African and western Mediterranean forms of *Testudo*. The information is not more specific as to the individual subspecies because there is so much ambiguity and uncertainty among the identification of the tortoises in this group. Unless you know the exact location of origin for your tortoises, it is nearly impossible for you to determine which subspecies or population you have. For information on the northern subspecies of *Testudo graeca*, refer to the entry on Greek tortoises in Chapter 7: Grassland Species.

Origin

Several subspecies of *T. graeca* occur from northern Morocco along the coast of North Africa to Libya. There is a large gap in the range, with the tortoises also being found in Israel north to Turkey and east to Iran. The species also has disjointed populations in southern Europe; tortoises from those areas are discussed in Chapter 7.

Most Greek tortoises are not found in Greece; there is a small portion of northeastern Greece that falls within the range of the northern subspecies. They get their common name from the pattern on the carapace, which is said to resemble a Grecian frieze. Greek tortoises are sometimes called spur-thighed tortoises, which can cause confusion with the sulcata tortoise because that species is often called the African spurred tortoise.

Habitat

These tortoises can be found in deserts to dry mountain habitats. They frequent areas within their range that have standing water available. Some local populations in Morocco and Syria live in higher elevations and might experience periods of hibernation. Most of those available to the average tortoise keeper originate at lower elevations in desert habitats with high temperatures and restricted rainfall.

Biology

The taxonomy of *Testudo graeca* is extremely complicated. Because the natural range is so fragmented, there may be little gene flow between populations, allowing distinct differences to develop between the populations. At least 20 subspecies have been named, and some of them are often recognized as separate species. They are confusingly similar and seem to interbreed occasionally in nature (and have been crossbred in captivity).

These tortoises range in size from a minimum of 7 inches (18 cm) for those found in Morocco and Tunisia to 9 inches (23 cm) for those found in the Middle East. They all have a very similar appearance: highly domed, with a flare to the back of shell. Those that occur in lowland desert areas tend to have little or no black pattern. The ones found at higher altitudes tend to have a greater amount of black, though the ones found in the north are usually not

Greek tortoises vary in color, size, and other attributes across their large range. These individuals originated in Libya.

solid black. These tortoises have enlarged conical scales on the back of the rear legs.

In North Africa this tortoise does not truly hibernate except for possibly at the higher altitudes. The tortoises do aestivate to escape the desert heat during the driest parts of the year, however. They do not normally dig burrows, but instead dig what are called pallets, small depressions in the earth that are usually situated at the base of a bush. They are not very deep. The tortoise will sometimes cover the front and back opening of the shell.

These tortoises are commonly the victim of cattle and goat herders, who place a bounty on their heads. In the past, herders would kill the tortoise on sight to make trinkets out of the shells. This has been frowned on in recent years, and the practice seems to be on the decline in much of the tortoise's natural range.

Captive Care

The desert-dwelling Greek tortoises are captive-bred fairly commonly, although not as frequently as northern grassland types. The desert forms tend to be a little more delicate than the grassland forms because most do not tolerate cold temperatures very well. Wild-caught African Greek tortoises often do not adapt to captivity because of parasites and anorexia—the latter likely due to the tortoise being imprinted on foods from its natural habitat.

The indoor setup for the desert *T. graeca* is not much different than the setup for other *Testudo* with the exception that the temperature should be maintained at a more restricted and stable range in the area of 80°F (26.5°C) with a basking place of at least 90°F (32°C) The humidity should be below 40 percent with a small humid section or hide of at least 80 percent humidity that the turtle can use as desired.

Greek tortoises are opportunistic feeders. They will consume carrion, insects, feces, and broadleaf weeds as their main diet. When greens

This darkly colored Greek tortoise is from Syria.

get scarce, they will consume grasses and hay and just about anything else they find. Because they are opportunistic feeders, they can overeat and thus are especially prone to putting on weight, giving the appearance of bags under the forward and hind legs. This should not be a problem if you are feeding a good varied diet.

If the tortoise is kept in a cooler climate, the normal behavior of building a pallet might not be sufficient to keep it healthy. A heated hide will be required when temperatures are under 50°F (10°C) if the tortoises are maintained outdoors.

The desert-dwelling Greek tortoises are not captive bred as often as the grassland types. This is a pair of *T. g. terrestris*.

One health issue to note: wild-caught North African *Testudo* seem to be frequent carriers of the herpes virus, which can be devastating to a group of tortoises. Extreme caution should be exercised when introducing one of these tortoises to an existing group.

Breeding

Breeding behavior is tied to the rainy season, as is the case with most desert-dwelling tortoises. Spring rains and the plant growth they trigger cue mating behavior in these tortoises in May, with nesting from May to June. In indoor setups, they respond to artificially created seasons of humidity, temperature, and food availability. If you provide them with a cool winter season, temperatures should not be allowed to drop below 60°F (15.5°C).

When North African *Testudo* breed, they are very vocal and active. Occasionally the female gets injured by the male, but this is not as common with the smaller southern races. In nature, eggs are deposited by the female in up to three nestings per season, and there are six to seven eggs in each nesting. The eggs usually weigh 10 to 15 grams each, but with larger eggs there are usually fewer deposited. Regardless of size, the eggs hatch in 60 to 75 days. In captivity, clutches may contain up to 10 eggs. They hatch in 60 to 80 days (occasionally as long as 90 days) when incubated at 80.5° to 88°F (27° to 31°C).

Recommendation

As with most other *Testudo*, these are great first tortoises. The only difficulty comes when the keeper obtains wild-caught individuals.

Russian Tortoise (*Testudo horsfieldii*)

Origin

The Russian tortoise has a very large home range: from Iran east to China, from the Gulf of Oman in the south to Russia in the north. Other names for this species include the steppe tortoise, the Central Asian tortoise, and Horsfield's tortoise. There is ongoing debate as to whether this species should be considered a member of *Testudo* or given its own genus, *Agrionemys*.

Habitat

The range of the Russian tortoise varies in habitat from desert to steppes. The steppe is a semi-arid grassland with very few trees. It has a mostly rocky substrate, with very little vegetation besides low weeds and grasses. It is characterized by extremely cold

Wild Russian tortoises are inactive during the frigid winters and blistering summers.

winters and equally extremely hot summers. The Russian tortoise is limited to an active season of only four to five months because of the harsh environment. The tortoise occupies oases, in addition to rivers and streams where it can find what limited green growth that might occur.

Biology

The Russian tortoise is as wide as it is long, giving it a nearly circular appearance when viewed from above. It attains a maximum length of 8 inches (20 cm). It has a relatively low flat profile. The color can be anywhere from yellow to all-black and everything in between; the dark color can be worn off by the constant burrowing. Most Russian tortoises out of the wild have a very rough and worn appearance. The plastron is usually black, with the growth between the scutes being yellow in color.

The only visible differences between the male and the female are that the male has a longer tail and is usually smaller than the female. The male does not have a concave plastron.

The Russian tortoise is an opportunistic feeder: it will eat all types of plant matter, along with occasional insects, carrion, and feces from other animals. The growth rate is reported to be extremely fast during the relatively short time it is active and feeding.

Russian tortoises come out of hibernation approximately in mid-March. The males will retreat back to their burrows around late May after breeding is complete. This corresponds with the very short rainy season. In late May, temperatures rise and the tortoises begin estivation. After the summer, they usually emerge from aestivation for a brief period of activity before winter sets in. The Russian tortoise is reported to dig long burrows in which it is protected from the heat and cold. The deep burrow also provides a humid environment, which reduces the loss of moisture and prevents dehydration. Once the tortoise enters the burrow it will seal off the burrow with dirt and debris, which protects the tortoise until the next season, when it will emerge to start the cycle all over again.

On emergence from hibernation, males immediately pursue females within their extremely limited home territory. It is during this time that the males and the females feed themselves almost nonstop. The tortoises have a small window of time in which to feed and breed.

The females will travel great distances to breed and lay eggs. The nesting period lasts roughly a month and a half, during which the female may nest more than one time. Females lay as many as five eggs at each nesting. The eggs hatch after approximately 100 days. The female seeks shelter after nesting is complete. The hatchlings will take up to five years before they develop the characteristic shape of the Russian tortoise.

Captive Care

The Russian tortoise does not have a record of doing well in captivity. Tortoises taken out of the wild are heavily infested with internal parasites. Exported tortoises can not withstand the stress of exportation or endure the parasite load, so the majority die in transit or shortly thereafter. With the arrival of farms that are breeding this species in conditions similar to their natural habitat, this will hopefully change.

Today there are many more captive-born Russian tortoises available than wild-caught ones. Captive-bred Russian tortoises are relatively easy to maintain in captivity.

The care of this species is similar to that of other desert-dwelling *Testudo*. However, a few cautions need to be mentioned. Russian tortoises tolerate the cold very well, provided that it is not damp. It is extremely important that the tortoise be allowed to dry out and not be exposed to constantly moist environments. The tortoise will benefit from a humid hide, but it should be warm to avoid any respiratory problems. If Russian tortoises are kept outdoors, the keeper should make sure the soil is well drained and allowed to dry out between watering the plants. In cooler climates, a lightly heated hide should be provided until the tortoise is ready to be taken inside—or allowed to hibernate should the keeper want to go that route.

Tortoises that come out of hibernation should be monitored to be sure they do not eat too much. If a pellet diet is used, it should be fed sparingly, perhaps only once or twice a week. Dark leafy greens can be fed as often as the animals like to fill in the gap. This diet should reduce any excessive rapid growth.

Russian tortoises are great escape artists. They not only can dig down beneath the enclosure walls but also are fantastic climbers. If a tortoise is missing, the keeper should dig around a missing pen before starting to panic. Russian tortoises have no trouble hooking their limbs over any kind of mesh or hand-hold to climb out of a pen. They can also wedge themselves between objects—such as where the walls of the enclosure meet in a corner—to climb up.

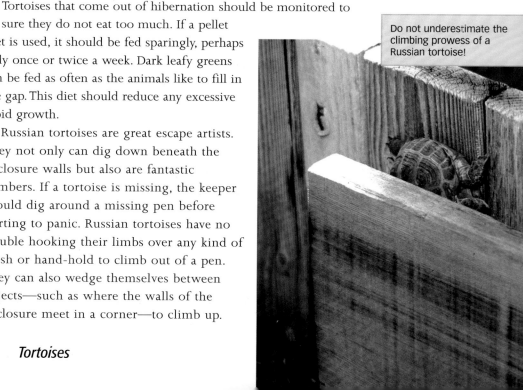

Do not underestimate the climbing prowess of a Russian tortoise!

Male (left) Russian tortoises do not have concave plastrons; their plastrons are flat like those of the females (right).

Breeding

It is recommended that the keeper hibernate Russian tortoises if they are expected to breed. Hibernation is not a requirement to induce breeding, but it does increase the chances of producing fertile eggs. Russian tortoises will usually breed shortly after emerging from hibernation in the spring when the weather starts to warm up. In captivity, the Russian tortoise that is breeding can be expected to lay from one to seven eggs that should hatch out in 60 to 90 days (up to 128 days at most) when incubated at a temperature of 80.5° to 88°F (27 to 31°C).

Recommendation

Wild-caught Russian tortoises should be left in the hands of expert keepers. Captive-bred turtles can make good pets for beginners, although you must make sure that conditions are not allowed to become too damp. Additionally, the temperatures cannot be allowed to get cool enough to induce hibernation unless the keeper is prepared for it.

Sulcata Tortoise (*Geochelone sulcata*)

Origin

Historically, sulcata tortoises ranged in Africa from Mauritania to Ethiopia, in a zone just below the Equator called the sub-Saharan Sahel. Currently it occurs only in fragmented populations throughout that range. This species is often called the African spurred tortoise. To avoid confusion with the Greek tortoise, also called the spur-thighed tortoise, this book refers to *G. sulcata* as the sulcata tortoise. The sulcata has recently been placed in the genus *Centrochelys*.

Habitat

The sub-Saharan Sahel is characterized by dry sandy soil and is occupied by low-lying shrubs and bushes such as acacias and other spiny plants. This region has a short rainy season that lasts from July to August, and a warm humid season that lasts from January to February. The remaining months of the year, the climate is hot and dry. The sulcata has adapted to this hostile environment by digging very long and deep burrows in which it can escape the harsh conditions.

Sulcatas dig extensive tunnels to escape extreme weather. In their natural habitat, many other animals take shelter in sulcata burrows.

Biology

The sulcata tortoise is the largest mainland tortoise: it can attain a weight of over 200 pounds (91 kg). It has a shape that varies from round to rectangular, with a relatively low profile well suited for digging and bulldozing the soil. The forelimbs have distinctly pointed overlapping scales, which is why is often called the African spurred tortoise. In the wild, the tortoise is a light straw color caused by sun bleaching.

During the hot dry periods the tortoise will spent long periods of time in its burrow. The burrow is deep enough to keep the tortoise cool and relatively moist, reducing water loss during respiration.

Wild sulcata tortoises consume almost anything they can fit into their mouths and are very opportunistic feeders. They primarily eat the usual hays and grasses, along with carrion, insects, and animal wastes.

There is a distinct difference between the male and the female, with the male being larger than the female. The male will have a noticeably longer tail and a distinctively concaved plastron. The female will have a flat plastron along with a short stubby tail.

Breeding takes place from November to May, just before the rainy season. Females can deposit up to four clutches in a season, with 10 to 30 eggs in each clutch. The eggs are golfball sized and take roughly 120 days to hatch, with a reported hatch rate of over 95 percent.

Captive Care

Sulcata tortoises are one of the easiest tortoises to care for, but it cannot be stressed strongly enough that this tortoise requires very careful consideration because of its great size and strength. This is especially true if the tortoise is being kept in a climate where it needs to be housed indoors for any length of time. Sulcatas are very forgiving tortoises, but only if the keeper can accommodate such a large and potentially destructive animal. They do need to feel secure, or they will be inclined to dig long burrows or push through fencing. A 200-pound (91-kg) tortoise can do this easily. The enclosure should be built of solid fencing, but in any case the enclosure walls should be buried deep enough so the tortoise cannot dig or push under it. A warm hide should also be provided.

Water is especially important to sulcata tortoises, for two main reasons. First, these tortoises have a renal system that makes them prone to bladder stones if the keeper is not careful. Secondly, sulcata tortoises maintained outdoors like to eat just about everything. Without good hydration and exercise, they are prone to gut impactions from things such as pine needles and pine cones, in addition to dried leaves and small branches. These items should not normally be of any real concern, but the keeper should be aware of this issue.

If a lawn or planted enclosure cannot be provided, the diet should be supplemented with good Bermuda hay or grass. Caution should be exercised when using a pelleted diet, because these tortoises like to gorge themselves. If fed too much of a rich diet, they can grow too quickly. The occasional ingestion of a dead animal, waste product, or insect should not be a concern.

The sulcata is covered in this chapter because it is found in a desert climate. That is not to say it cannot tolerate a humid environment. The only caveat is to make sure the tortoise can escape the humidity. These tortoises are also very cold-tolerant as long as the ambient atmosphere is not humid. They require supplemental heating for temperatures below 50°F (10°C).

Sulcatas are the third largest species of tortoise. They are too big for indoor housing under most circumstances.

Breeding

The sulcata is just as prolific a breeder in captivity as it is in the wild. In the warmer climates it usually breeds in the springtime, with the arrival of the rainy season to promote good plant growth. The rainy season can vary from region to region; the tortoise is normally able to adjust.

In most cases the tortoise should not be encouraged to dig a burrow. A sandy area should be provided in a sunny portion of the yard, which the tortoise can hopefully be encouraged to use as a nesting site. The sulcata tortoise is quite consistent in the style of nest it builds. It will first dig a pre-nest and then dig the cavity to hold the eggs. The eggs can be buried quite deeply.

The female can deposit up to 34 eggs, with 17 being the typical clutch size. The eggs should be expected to hatch between 81 and 170 days but may take up to 210 days. The incubation temperature should be between 80.5° and 88°F (27 and 31°C). When the hatchlings emerge, they are light brown in color, with the new growth coming in as a dark chocolate brown, which lightens over time. The faster the growth the longer it will take for this color to lighten. There are color morphs, such as albinos or others that lack pigment. The new growth on these tortoises will not come in dark.

Recommendation

The sulcata is a hardy, impressive, and personable tortoise, but because of its enormous size it is usually a poor choice for beginners. Reptile rescues and animal shelters now often have sulcatas in their care because keepers were unprepared for the turtle's size and abandoned them.

Hacthling sulcata tortoises are commonly available at reptile expos.

The Desert Tortoise of the American Southwest

The desert tortoise (*Gopherus agassizii*) is one of the most well-recognized tortoises in the world among tortoise keepers, because it is so well studied and publicized. It can be found from the Mojave Desert southward to Sonora, Mexico, and east to Arizona. It inhabits a specific area in those deserts, characterized by very well-drained sand associated with alluvial plains or desert washes. Alluvial plains are areas of material that is washed down desert canyons to the desert floor. They are areas that usually have a rich spring flora that attracts the desert tortoises and other desert herbivores. These areas also attract desert tourists looking for the flowers and wildlife, which sometimes include the tortoises.

In years past people collected these tortoises, even though it was illegal. Some even used them for target practice. While both of these practices have slowed dramatically, they still do occur. Some believe there are more desert tortoises in backyards than in the wild.

It is against the law to collect these tortoises, but it is not against the law to own them in the states of origin, provided the keeper is a state resident and the proper permits have been obtained. Desert tortoises make great pets, but they do not handle change very well. When removed from their comfort zone they usually do not thrive. The best thing a keeper can do, when presented with the opportunity to adopt one of these tortoises, is to carefully consider where it is coming from and where it will end up being kept. Desert tortoises like warm and dry conditions. Hatchlings can be set up indoors on a very limited basis. It is not recommended to even try to keep an adult indoors. While the desert tortoise does have a limited range and availability, quite a few hobbyists in the American Southwest keep them, and they do come up for adoption relatively frequently.

Geochelone pardalis

Chapter 7

Grassland Species

T his chapter discusses the tortoises that naturally inhabit open grassy terrain. Most of these species are found in areas with few trees but with abundant grasses, bushes, and shrubs. Most of the habitats are rather arid, although not as arid as a true desert. The grassland species include some commonly kept tortoises, such as the leopard and Hermann's tortoises, as well as the much rarer pancake tortoise.

Included here are two species—the Aldabra tortoise and the red-footed tortoise—that range over a variety of habitats. They have been placed in this chapter because they are most often found in grassy open areas bordering forests. Unlike the other species covered here, these two hail from humid environments, and they require more humid keeping conditions.

Aldabra Tortoise (*Geochelone gigantea*)

Origin

The only natural population of Aldabra tortoise occurs on the island of Aldabra, a small atoll in the Indian Ocean northeast of Madagascar. It is part of the Seychelles Islands. There are captive breeding populations on some of the other Seychelles Islands, in addition to Mauritius and Zanzibar Island in the Indian Ocean. The taxonomic status of the Aldabra tortoise is in flux, and it is sometimes found under the names *Aldabrachelys gigantea* and *Dipsochelys dussumieri*.

Habitat

In its natural environment, the Aldabra tortoise occupies most of the available habitat on its small island home. Aldabra is relatively flat, with its highest point being only 26 feet (8 m) above sea level. The habitats that are available to the tortoise are grasslands, along with scrubland, mangrove forests, and beaches. From November to March the island receives the heaviest rainfall. The mean annual rainfall of 26.5 inches (670 mm), but there can be drastic variation depending on a particular monsoon season. Temperature varies with little the seasons. The summer high temperature is an average maximum of 90°F (32°C) and the winter average low temperature is a minimum of 72°F (22°C).

The Aldabra tortoise is one of the truly giant species and can reach a length greater than 43 inches (109 cm).

Other Grassland Tortoises

Much of the care and breeding information detailed in this chapter can be applied to other species that are found in similar habitats. These include the Texas tortoise (*Gopherus berlandieri*) from the United States and Mexico, as well as many of the South African tortoises, such as the geometric and tent tortoises (*Psammobates* species) and the bowsprit or angulated tortoise (*Chersina angulata*). None of these species is particularly common in the hobby, although they are kept by hobbyists living within their natural range.

Marginated tortoises (*Testudo marginata*) are now being bred in reasonable numbers and do well when kept as a grassland species. The species is native to a small area of Greece and possibly Albania but has been introduced to several other parts of Europe. The star tortoise (*Geochelone elegans*) of India and Sri Lanka is occasionally available and should be kept as a grassland species. The spider tortoise (*Pyxis arachnoides*) inhabits thorny scrub forests in southern Madagascar. It should be kept like a grassland species but, like the redfoot and Aldabra tortoises, requires higher humidity than the other species. Another Madagascar species, the radiated tortoise (*Geochelone radiata*), can be kept in the same fashion as the leopard tortoise. The endangered and rarely available Galapagos giant tortoise (*Chelonoidis nigra*) can be kept in the same fashion as the Aldabra.

Spider tortoise

World Heritage Site

Aldabra Atoll has been designated a World Heritage Site by the United Nations Educational, Scientific, and Cultural Organization (UNESCO) because of its unique flora and fauna. This designation provides the tortoises and other wildlife with protection from exploitation. The number of people allowed to visit the island is highly regulated, and there are no permanent human residents.

Biology

The carapace of the Aldabra tortoise is high domed, and both the plastron and carapace are black in color. The plastron has no distinguishing marks. The most distinguishing features are the relatively pointy head and the elongated, elliptical nasal openings. A small nuchal scute usually is present. The Aldabra tortoise is a truly giant tortoise; it can attain a size of more than 43 inches (109 cm) SCL and a weight of more than 330 pounds (150 kg). Males are normally larger than the females and usually will be more elongated in shape. Males have long tails and concave plastrons, while females have short tails and flat plastrons. These traits may not be readily apparent on tortoises that weigh less than 250 pounds (113 kg).

In the wild the Aldabra tortoise occupies all the habitats it has available but shows a preference for the grasslands along where it does most of its feeding and foraging. It is similar to other tortoises in that it is mainly herbivorous but feeds opportunistically on animal matter.

The habitat does not provide an abundance of food for the tortoises. They consume most of the plant species that occur in the habitat but seem to prefer grasses. Grazing by Aldabra tortoises has forced the plants to adapt, so they have become dwarfed and produce seeds close to the ground to avoid their consumption. This mix of dwarfed plant species is called tortoise turf and is composed of grasses, sedges, and some broad-leafed plants. The Aldabra tortoise will feed on carrion including the carcasses of other Aldabra tortoises. In the wet seasons, Aldabras obtain water from the pools that form from rainfall. When there is no rainfall, the tortoises obtain their moisture from food items.

Mating takes place from February to May. Females nest in the months of June through September, which is the dry season. The female will dig a typical flask-shaped nest, and nesting usually takes place at dusk or at night. The tortoise deposits from 5 to14 eggs. Females living in high population density lay fewer eggs than those living in less dense populations. The eggs are hard-shelled, round in shape, and 48 to 51 mm in diameter. These eggs take 98 to 200 days to hatch, so the hatchlings emerge in the rainy season from October to December.

When the tortoises emerge they fend for themselves. Mortality is reported to be high due to predation by coconut crabs and introduced rats. The young tortoises grow rapidly and quickly become too large for any of the natural predators on the island.

Captive Care

There are a few successful Aldabra tortoise breeders throughout the world. The species is available but only in small numbers, making them expensive tortoises rarely available to the average hobbyist. The Aldabra is covered here because it is a wonderful species to keep and a well-known and highly desired species.

Aldabra tortoises are easy to care for provided the keeper is prepared for the enormous size adult size of this species. The most challenging aspect is the housing of adults. If the keeper does not live in a warm climate, this can be a daunting task—few keepers have the space for an indoor Aldabra enclosure. Aldabras do very well in a large well-planted yard. Most of the plant should be grasses, with some stout shrubs and trees for shade. These tortoises enjoy soaking, so it's best to provide a pond in the pen. Although this species is quite tolerant of cool temperatures, they should have access to supplemental heating whenever the temperature drops below 75°F (24°C). Using a heated shed is the best way to provide supplemental heating to these giants.

Diet should consist mainly of grasses and hays, but an Aldabra will readily forage throughout its enclosure on anything it can consume, including dried leaves and the bark off branches. Vegetables and greens can supplement the grass and hay. Pellet diets are recommended because they were specifically designed for these large tortoise species and provide good nutrition for healthy development. However, it is probably best to limit feeding pellets to no more than twice weekly. This should be supplemented with

Size comparison between two-year-old and eight-year-old Aldabra tortoises.

Aldabras enjoy having ponds or large puddles to soak in on hot days.

calcium carbonate because the calcium requirement for the Aldabra tortoise is quite high. Another recommended supplement for these large tortoises is kelp, which is high in iodine. The larger tortoises are susceptible to thyroid gland problems, and the additional iodine seems to help prevent their occurrence.

Breeding

Breeding of the Aldabra tortoise mostly has been limited to those areas near their natural range, such as islands in the Indian Ocean near Madagascar. In such locales, the breeding pattern can follow the same environmental cycles as on Aldabra. There have been some recent breedings of the Aldabra tortoise in the United States, but these not been very well documented.

Recommendation

The Aldabra tortoise is a fantastic tortoise that is easy to keep provided the keeper understands how to manage such a large animal. A 300- to 400-pound (136- to 181-kg) tortoise is not the same as a small *Testudo*. There are additional considerations, such as the size and strength of the housing and how to make provisions for veterinary care. This tortoise does not do well indoors full time, so if outdoors provisions cannot be provided at least seven months out of the year a keeper should seek a more manageable species.

Bell's Hinge-Backed Tortoise (*Kinixys belliana*)

Origin
There are two distinct populations of Bell's hinge-backed tortoise in Africa. The western population is found from Senegal to Nigeria. The remaining population is found from Sudan to southern Democratic Republic of Congo, extending south to Angola and east to Swaziland. There is an introduced population that is established in Madagascar.

Habitat
Although the range of Bell's hinge-backed tortoise is quite extensive, the habitat it prefers appears to be quite consistent. Throughout its range it can be found from the edges of dry forests to savannahs dominated by grass and thorny scrub. These areas border more moist habitats, and there are distinct wet and dry seasons throughout this range.

Biology
Bell's hinge-backed tortoises are elongated in shape. They usually are dark brown, with a slightly lighter radiated or speckled pattern. There is much variation across the enormous natural range. Bell's hingebacks can reach a length of just over 8.5 inches (21.5 cm).

Bell's hingeback has an enormous natural range covering much of Sub-Saharan Africa.

The most distinctive feature of the genus *Kinixys* is the hinged rear carapace, which allows the back of the carapace to close in with the plastron to conceal the tail area. The tortoise is able to do this because of the presence of two soft hinge points situated just in front of the hind leg

pockets and extending up the vertical side of the carapace. The hinge does not extend across the top of the carapace. The flat portion of the carapace allows the flexing of the top of the shell with the aid of the hinges.

This is a particularly brightly colored Bell's hingeback that was photographed in Mozambique.

The male is distinguished from the female by being smaller in size. The male also has a much longer tail than the female. The male does not have a concave plastron. The female usually has a slightly widened posterior carapace.

The two populations are thought to be two separate subspecies. *Kinixys belliana belliana* is the eastern population and *Kinixys belliana nogueyi* is the western population. They can be differentiated by the number of claws on the front feet. *Kinixys b. belliana* will usually have five claws on the front feet, and *Kinixys b. nogueyi* will have only four claws on the front feet. It is commonly believed that the two subspecies are actually separate species.

The western population occurs mostly along forest edges where the humidity is high but the climate is not overly wet. The eastern population of Bell's hinge-backed tortoise mostly occupies a dry grassland habitat where it is most active during the wetter parts of the year. Both populations prefer a moist micro-habitat during their active periods. During the dry seasons both populations will estivate in animal burrows or burrow into leaf litter or other cover that will retain moisture. Hingebacks do not normally dig their own burrows but have been known to dig into termite mounds to escape the dry periods. They will remain under cover until they perceive signs that the rains are returning, at which time they will emerge and resume foraging. Atmospheric pressure is thought to be one of the signs that tortoises respond to.

This is one tortoise that is truly omnivorous in nature. It consumes carrion, along with snails, slugs, millipedes, insects, and worms. It will also devour various mushrooms and other fungi, and these items seem to be a favored food of this species. When foraging on plant matter the hingeback focuses on the broadleaf weeds and moist grasses; it is reported to also feed on fallen fruit in nature. The tortoise is partially crepuscular (active at twilight) in its habits, as it is most active during the late afternoon to the evening after sunset.

Breeding usually takes place during the rainy season when the tortoise emerges from estivation. Males will hunt for females and engage in combat when another male is encountered. One male will commonly flip the other male onto its back, from which position it will quickly recover and right itself. When a receptive female is encountered the male will mount the female from the rear. Usually the male will be in an almost vertical position, as if he were standing on the back end of his shell (This is very similar to the mating position of North American box turtles).

Eggs are typically deposited in the summer, which is from November to April. The female can deposit multiple clutches of eggs, with a normal clutch ranging from two to seven eggs. Incubation normally takes 90 to 110 days, but hatchlings have been discovered during the months March to April. The West African Bell's hingeback is said to produce smaller clutches of two to four eggs.

Captive Care

Bell's hingeback is no longer commonly available, but it once was imported in huge numbers. Importation of this species into the United States was banned because the ticks found on the turtles possibly carried heartwater, a serious cattle disease. Although there are still long-term captive wild-caught Bell's in the hobby, most of those available in the United States are captive-bred.

There are some key points concerning the captive care of Bell's hinge-backed tortoise. When setting up the enclosure it is recommended that the keeper make sure there is a humid hide and also a place where the tortoise

Bell's hingeback is rarely bred in captivity. This is a juvenile.

can dry out. This is especially important with an outdoor enclosure. These tortoises are very active in the early evening hours. They are good climbers, so be certain to make sure that all escape routes are properly blocked. An overhanging lip and a buried barrier under the fence will help prevent escapes.

When feeding a Bell's, it is important to include animal matter in the form of insects.

Speke's Hingeback

A species that is similar to the Bell's hingeback and is also occasionally available is Speke's hingeback (*Kinixys spekii*). This tortoise was considered a subspecies of *Kinixys belliana* until fairly recently. Wild-caught Speke's hingebacks are still imported but are best avoided because of their poor chance of survival. Captive breeding of Speke's hingeback seems to be increasing but is still rare. The care for this species is more or less the same as that for Bell's hingeback.

That not only stimulates the tortoise to be more active as it hunts for the prey but also seems to be beneficial to it. You can also feed these tortoises occasional pinky mice and snails. This species seems to enjoy fungi such as mushrooms, just as it does in the wild. The mushrooms might serve a beneficial purpose, so you should include them in the diet frequently. You should also add a small amount of fruit to the diet. Bell's hingeback seems to do well on a pelleted diet fed in addition to the items mentioned previously.

Breeding

In warmer climates Bell's hingeback will usually acclimate to the local conditions when it comes to breeding. If it is given a cool-down period or a dry season, it will usually breed on emerging from this period. In captivity females can deposit two to four eggs, which should hatch in approximately 123 days at a temperature of 77° to 86°F (25° to 30° C). These numbers can vary considerably; this species has not been frequently bred in captivity, so the reasons behind the variations in egg incubation are not fully understood.

Recommendation

Bell's hingebacks have some unique characteristics that can make them very interesting pets. Because breeding is so uncommon, advanced hobbyists can contribute to the knowledge pool by attempting to breed this species and sharing the results. Captive-bred Bell's hingebacks would be suitable for new tortoise keepers, but they are rarely available.

European Greek Tortoise (*Testudo graeca*)

Note that this entry is only for the subspecies of *T. graeca* found on the northern coast of the Mediterranean Sea. For information on the other subspecies of *Testudo graeca*, refer to the entry on Greek tortoises in Chapter 6: Desert Species.

Origin

A number of subspecies of the Greek tortoise are found in countries on the northern Mediterranean coast, although not nearly as many as are found in North Africa and the Middle East. Two of these are commonly kept as pets: *T. g. graeca* and *T. g. ibera*. *Testudo g. graeca* is found on the coast of southern Spain, and *Testudo g. ibera*—often considered a separate species and named *Testudo ibera*—occurs in northeastern Greece, Romania, Bulgaria, Turkey, and much of the Caucasus region.

Habitat

These tortoises typically inhabit dry rocky areas that are almost desert-like but differ from true deserts in that they receive more rainfall. Other habitats that are used by them include rolling hillsides, valleys, and plains. Such areas do have grasses, shrubs, and some trees unless they have been cultivated. Many tortoise populations have gravitated towards cultivated fields and grasslands used for grazing because of the abundance of rich green forage.

The rainy season is typically in the spring, with occasional light rains in the northern part of the range depending on the topography of the region. These rains typically produce lush temporary growth. In the southernmost parts of the range in Spain, the habitat is similar to coastal northwest Africa.

Biology

The northern Mediterranean group of *Testudo greaca* is made up of several subspecies, and the taxonomy of this group is always in flux. Some are currently considered by some to be individual species, such as *Testudo graeca* and *Testudo ibera*. In other cases, some former subspecies are now regarded as localized variants. As previously mentioned, individuals of these subspecies and variants can be very difficult to distinguish from

Testudo greaca ibera is one of the largest of the Mediterranean tortoises and may grow to be 10 inches (25 cm) or more in length.

each other visually. However, *T. g. graeca* and *T. g. ibera* are exceptions and can be distinguished without too much difficulty.

Testudo graeca graeca is a small tortoise that reaches an SCL of 8 to 10 inches (20 to 25.5 cm). It is very similar to *T. graeca* found in northwest coastal Africa. It has a mottled pattern and highly domed carapace. The base color is yellow to orange to dark brown. It occurs only in the coastal areas of Spain and some isolated islands.

These tortoises normally do not hibernate but do experience winter and summer rest periods. Breeding and egg-laying of this particular population follows that of the northwest coastal African population: Breeding takes place in early spring with the onset of rains, and egg-laying takes part in early summer.

Testudo graeca ibera is one of the largest of the *Testudo graeca* group; it can attain a length of over 10 cm (25 cm). There are anecdotal reports of some populations in Turkey that can get much larger than this. Older individuals are usually very dark in color, with some light mottling sometimes present. The base color can be olive green to dark brown. Younger individuals will have a black radiating pattern on each carapace scute. The habitat this tortoise occupies is normally long rolling hills and grassy plains. This appears to be one of those tortoises that seem to have benefited from the cultivation of fields for the grazing of cattle. As with most of the others in the *Testudo* group, they are highly opportunistic feeders. It is not uncommon for them to take animal matter such as carrion or insects although they are typically herbivorous in nature.

Testudo g. ibera does hibernate during the winter months of November to February and will estivate during the hottest summer periods. Breeding takes place in the months of March and April, after hibernation, with nesting typically taking place in May to June. Mating can be quite violent, as is typical with the *Testudo* group. *Testudo g. ibera* is known to produce multiple nests; some of those nests are produced

Wild Greek tortoise photographed in southwestern Turkey.

Young Greek tortoises have a soft shell when they hatch; it hardens up within the first few years of the turtle's life.

so late in the year that the eggs will over-winter in the nest to hatch the following spring. This usually happens in the extreme northern populations. The female will normally deposit four or five eggs at each nesting.

Captive Care

Although Greek tortoises are rarely imported into the pet trade as wild-caught animals, captive-born animals are readily available in the United States and Europe. Greek tortoises have been bred in captivity for multiple generations. This is true more so in Europe, but they are becoming more popular and available in the United States.

Care for the hatchlings follows the same general guidelines as the care for other grassland species. The keeper needs to be careful selecting plants and produce if feeding a green-based diet. Fruits and watery vegetables are not recommended unless they are fed in very limited portions. Excess feeding of those items will lead to watery feces. A pelleted diet combined with a dark leafy green diet is recommended for the hatchling tortoise.

Daily soaking or providing a small water dish is essential for these tortoises, as it is with most others.

As the tortoise grows, be aware of its shell hardness. These tortoises typically do not start developing hard shells for a few years. If the shell does not harden up after that, examine the care and feeding to make sure that proper calcium and UVB are provided.

Greek tortoises are excellent burrowers, so provision should be made to prevent them from tunneling out of an enclosure. *Testudo graeca* is also very well adapted for climbing, which should be taken into account when constructing a fence or wall.

Hibernation is a hotly debated topic as regards the extreme northern populations of European tortoises. *Testudo g. ibera* does hibernate in the winter, and the eggs sometimes over-winter in the nest. It is important to remember that the tortoise has more control in nature

The European varieties of the Greek tortoise are frequently captive bred.

and instinctually chooses the best hibernation spot it can find. Even so, some do not make it through hibernation. A tortoise hibernates in nature because it has no other choice. In captivity the proper care is provided by the keeper, so there is no physical reason for the tortoise to hibernate unless breeding is the goal. It is for this reason that hatchlings and juvenile tortoises should not be subjected to the risks of hibernation unnecessarily.

If these tortoises are kept outdoors, they can be hibernated naturally if the local climate allows enough of a drop in temperature to facilitate a natural hibernation. Care must be exercised for those being kept in climates where the temperature drops below freezing. In those cases, the tortoise must be able to dig a burrow deeper than the local frost line. Otherwise it is best to hibernate this species indoors.

Breeding

As with other *Testudo*, breeding in Greek tortoises commences after hibernation. Females lay five to ten eggs per clutch. They will hatch in 65 to 80 days when incubated at temperatures of 80.5° to 88°F (27° to 31°C).

Recommendation

All of the tortoises in the *Testudo graeca* group are highly recommended because they have a range in size and color that will appeal to any tortoise fan. All of the species in this group are highly animated, and captive-bred hatchlings are fairly easy to care for.

Hermann's Tortoise (*Testudo hermanni*)

Origin

Hermann's tortoise occurs across coastal southern Europe. The range is divided into three populations, although some mixing between the populations does occur. The western population occurs in coastal Italy, Corsica, Sardinia, Sicily, the Balearic Islands, and southeastern France. Several isolated populations exist in southeastern Spain. The eastern population is found across the Adriatic Sea from Albania to Bulgaria to the coast of the Black Sea. The range runs from southern Romania and Serbia south to southern Greece. A small population between the eastern and western populations is located from Montenegro along the Croatian coast up to the Slovenian border. The different populations may or may not be distinct subspecies.

Habitat

The common habitats for all three populations of Hermann's tortoise are locally known as *garrigue* and *maquis*. The *garrigue* is dominated by scattered trees and low-lying shrubs covering coastal hillsides. It is further classified as a scrubland dominated by evergreen trees and soft-leaved shrubs. There is not much ground cover below the main canopy in this habitat. The soil type consists mostly of weathered limestone. This habitat provides cover for

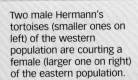

Two male Hermann's tortoises (smaller ones on left) of the western population are courting a female (larger one on right) of the eastern population.

the tortoise that would normally be impassable to a person. Growth of the prevailing flora is directly influenced by the surrounding waters and the available nutrients from the soil. Where the cover has been disturbed or partially cleared the habitat is called *maquis*, which very similar to the *garrique* but with more grasses and low ground cover along with dense clusters of evergreen shrubs.

Biology

Hermann's tortoises can be distinguished from the other species of *Testudo* by a horny claw-like scale on the tip of the tail, and both males and females possess this structure. Because the male's tail is thinner and longer the horny claw is much more pronounced and obvious. In the female the scale is there but not as obvious. The shell is a yellow to olive green color with a radiating black pattern on each scute. Wild-caught tortoises—as well as those kept outdoors—tend to have a less obvious pattern because the tortoise likes to dig, causing wear the shell. The radiated pattern becomes more of a mottled pattern similar to that of *Testudo graeca*. In all forms of Hermann's tortoise, the adult male is normally smaller than the female. The male is bell-shaped when viewed from above, while the female is more oval in shape.

Some authorities recognize two subspecies of Hermann's tortoise, and some recognize three. However, all would agree that the characteristics for distinguishing the differences between the three forms are inconsistent at best. The two forms that are the easiest to distinguish are the western and eastern forms. Note that this is true for adults only. Adult eastern Hermann's tortoise (*Testudo hermanni boettgeri*) is normally larger, and the female is more flattened than the western. The easterns tend to be brighter yellow than westerns. The western Hermann's tortoise (*Testudo hermanni hermanni*) is smaller, and the female is more dome-shaped. The colors tend to be dark and more greenish. The only way to distinguish the Dalmatian tortoise (*Testudo hermanni hercegovinensis*) is to know where it came from. There is still interbreeding between the populations, most notably between the Dalmatian and eastern, and this makes identification of the subspecies more difficult.

All three forms hibernate throughout their natural range. Certain populations will

This Hermann's tortoise is heading into its heated shed for the night. This species does well in outdoor housing.

Hermann's tortoises burrow extensively. To prevent escapes, sink the enclosure walls at least 6 inches (15 cm) into the ground.

estivate to escape the heat of the warmest part of the year. They normally hibernate within the months of October and March, but this will vary depending on how far north the population is, along with the influence of proximity to water and the altitude. Southern populations may emerge from hibernation temporarily during unseasonably warm periods. Various methods of hibernation are used by the tortoise, including burying and seeking refuge in rock outcroppings.

Hibernation normally ends with the arrival of spring rains, normally appearing from March to June. The tortoises immediately embark on courtship and mating. Eggs are deposited from June throughout the summer if the weather permits it. Females are capable of nesting multiple times and usually can produce up to three nests. A clutch can have from one to five eggs. Hatchling tortoises emerge in approximately 90 days, usually corresponding to the summer rains in August to September. During times of unusually dry weather the hatchlings may remain in the ground and over-winter in the nest, emerging with the spring rains. The abundant cover of the habitat seems to favor survival of the hatchling tortoises. Sexual maturity is reached in approximately 10 years for the male and approximately 13 years for the female.

Hermann's tortoise is mostly herbivorous, but it is pretty well documented that it feeds opportunistically on carrion and other animal matter. The majority of the diet is broadleaf plants.

Captive Care

Hermann's tortoise has become a very popular tortoise among tortoise keepers because it readily adapts to many environments and is a hardy tortoise. Many keepers are producing this

Hermann's tortoise breeds readily in captivity, and the species has become widely available.

species in both the United States and Europe, which makes individuals relatively easy to obtain without being too expensive. Some tortoise farms in Europe are producing Hermann's tortoises in massive numbers. The nice thing about these farms is that they are raising the tortoises past the critical hatchling stage, which makes the new keeper's job of raising them less stressful. Many of these tortoises are large enough to sex, so it is fairly easy to obtain pairs.

Farm-raised tortoises should be thoroughly checked by a veterinarian for parasites and other health issues.

Housing requires a special note with Hermann's tortoises, especially the easterns. These tortoises are excellent climbers and burrowers—better than even most other *Testudo*—which means any outdoor housing should be secured accordingly. The feeding recommendations are the same as for most other Mediterranean tortoises: mostly grasses and leafy greens, supplemented with occasional fruit. This regimen can possibly be mixed with a pelleted diet.

Breeding

Breeding in captivity follows the same patterns that are displayed in the wild. The tortoises normally breed during the spring wet season following the winter dormancy period. Hermann's tortoise can be hibernated outdoors, but the keeper must not allow the tortoise to experience temperatures below freezing. It can be expected to show breeding activity on the first few warm days after hibernation. If the mating is successful, the female may nest two or three times during the course of the summer. Western Hermann's tortoise females deposit four to five eggs per clutch, which will hatch in 60 to 66 days at an incubation temperature of 82.5° to 88°F (28° to 31°). Eastern Hermann's tortoises can lay up to 17 eggs in a clutch, and they will hatch in 54 to 79 days at an incubation temperature of 82.5° to 88°F (28° to 31°).

Recommendation

The hardiness, adaptability, personality, and availability of Hermann's tortoise make it the ideal tortoise for the new tortoise keeper.

Leopard Tortoise (*Geochelone pardalis*)

Origin

The leopard tortoise occurs throughout South Africa north to Angola. In the eastern part of its range it occurs throughout the Great Rift Valley north to Ethiopia and southern Sudan. The leopard tortoise is often placed in its own genus, *Stigmochelys*.

Habitat

Grasslands and thorn scrub are the primary habitats of the leopard tortoise, but it can be found on rocky hillsides and in thick shrublands as well. What these habitats have in common is that they have distinct wet and dry seasons with periods of lush growth and high humidity followed by very low humidity and a die-off of vegetation. The leopard tortoise can be found from sea level to altitudes of over 8,200 feet (2,500 m).

Leopard tortoises are found in grasslands, scrub forests, and semi-deserts across much of eastern and southern Africa.

Biology

The most obvious characteristic of the leopard tortoise is the distinctive spots, from which the leopard tortoise derives its common name. They have splashes of black on the pale yellow

It is fairly common for wild leopard tortoises to have pyramided shells.

color of the shell. The shell of the leopard tortoise is highly domed in most of the population, but there are isolated groups that are more flattened. In those populations the male is commonly more flat than the female. The rear marginal scutes are lightly flared and scalloped.

The leopard tortoise is one of the largest existing tortoise species. It can grow to a weight of over 110 pounds (50 kg), although it more commonly weighs 22 to 33 pounds (10 to 15 kg). Individuals are normally 16 to 20 inches (40.5 to 51 cm) in length.

The male is usually more elongated than the female. The tail of the male is much longer than that of the female. The plastron of the male is concave, but the plastron of the female is more flat. The female leopard tortoise is normally larger than the male except in some populations from the northern portion of its range where the opposite is true. The anal scutes of the male commonly form a V shape, and the anal scutes of the female usually form a U shape in which the tail protrudes from the shell, but this can vary between individuals.

In the past, herpetologists recognized two subspecies of the leopard tortoise. Those found in South Africa and southern Namibia were called *Geochelone pardalis pardalis*, and those in the rest of the range were called *Geohelone pardalis babcocki*. They are both now classified as *Geochelone pardalis*. As adults, the only distinguishing factor was the size of the tortoise, with those found in the south growing to a much larger size. However, very large tortoises have now been found throughout the range. Other than the size of the adults, it is very difficult to distinguish the two by appearance alone. As hatchlings, the two forms are relatively easy to distinguish. Hatchling tortoises of the southern form will have multiple spots on each scute, whereas hatchlings of the northern form will have single or no spots on each scute. There does seem to be some integration of the two forms, producing hatchlings displaying some scutes with multiple spots and other scutes that have one or none. The differences are too inconsistent to support formal recognition of subspecies, although hobbyists still use the names.

Leopard tortoises are normally diurnal in nature, and they are most active during the cooler times of the day—most often the early morning and late afternoon. When temperatures get too cold or too hot, they will hibernate or estivate depending on the local conditions. The tortoise is extremely adaptable, which could be a good reason for its extensive range.

When leopard tortoises are active they are always on the move foraging for anything they can find. It is well documented that these tortoises are avid swimmers, which is a needed survival trait because portions of their range experience seasonal flooding. Leopard tortoises feed mostly on grasses and other low-lying plants and shrubs. They will eat feces and carrion if they should come across it.

Breeding takes place during the warm season, which is between September and April in most of the range. Winter runs from June through August in South Africa, and tortoises in this area will hibernate during extended cold periods. This is also true of the leopards living at higher altitudes. In the populations that hibernate, the tortoises breed soon after emerging. Throughout the rest of the leopard tortoise's range eggs are deposited anytime during the warm season.

Both male and females can be extremely aggressive to both members of the opposite sex and their own sex. The female leopard tortoise can

Wild-caught juvenile leopard tortoise. This species is no longer imported because of concerns over tick-borne disease.

Grassland Species   **159**

deposit anywhere from 4 to 25 eggs, depending on the size of the tortoise. Leopards can nest up to seven times a year. The eggs will typically hatch in 120 to 200 days, the duration of the hatching period seeming to be dependent on local rainfall and temperatures.

Captive Care

Even though leopards are extremely adaptable in the wild, individuals imported in the past did not adapt to captivity very well. They used to be imported by the thousands, but recent legislation has stopped importation into the United States because leopard tortoises carried ticks that could pass heartwater disease on to cattle. The European community as well has slowed the importation drastically. Those leopards that did adapt to captivity did so very well and are reproducing in enormous numbers. Hatchling leopards are commonly available. Leopards are also being raised on tortoise farms within their natural range, but they cannot be imported into the United States.

Captive-raised three-year-old leopard tortoise. This species has been prolific in captivity.

Well-established leopard tortoises adapt well to most climates as long as it does not get too cold. Leopards should not be kept outdoors if the temperature goes below 55°F (13°C) and will need supplemental heat when temperatures drop below 75°F (24°C). Leopard tortoises do very well in high humidity as long as it is warm. They quickly develop respiratory problems if it is cool and damp. It is for this reason that leopard tortoises are recommended only for those in warmer climates.

Leopard tortoises need a diet of leafy greens and a high-quality pellet, supplemented with Bermuda hay or another good hay. If a well-planted yard is provided, no further supplements are needed besides the pellets once or twice a week, although providing a calcium supplement is a good idea. Leopard tortoises seem to be prone to pyramiding, and pyramided turtles occur frequently in nature. The condition can be minimized by providing proper heat and hydration with an excellent varied diet. It is important to note that the quantity of the food has nothing to do with pyramiding, but good food quality will help prevent or reduce it.

Breeding

Breeding in captivity follows most tortoise patterns in that the leopard tortoise will normally breed as long as it is warm. In warm regions breeding can take place during as many as nine months out of the year, with the tortoise nesting approximately every 30 days. A female normally produces 3 to 19 eggs but can produce up to 30 eggs in a clutch, depending on the size of the tortoise. The eggs will normally hatch in 120 to 200 eggs at a temperature of 82.5° to 86°F (28° to 30°C). There are records of the eggs of this species taking more than 400 days to hatch, but that is not a very common occurrence.

Recommendation

Leopard tortoises are extremely rewarding tortoises to keep but can be delicate if they are not kept under the correct conditions. They are not recommended for keepers who live in colder climates, because their large size makes them difficult to maintain indoors.

Pancake Tortoise (*Malacochersus tornieri*)

Origin

The pancake tortoise has an extremely limited range in Africa, where it occurs in southern Kenya and northern Tanzania.

The pancake tortoise gets its common name from its flattened body shape, an adaptation to squeezing into rocky crevices.

Habitat

This tortoise has both a limited range and a restricted habitat. It is found only on isolated rock outcroppings called *kopjes*. These rock outcroppings are unique in that they rise out of plains like islands and are isolated from each other.

The general conditions of the range are arid scrub with large rocks (mostly flat or round in shape) among sparse vegetation, aside from grasses and low-growing weeds. The altitude is over 5,900 feet (1798 m). There is relatively low rainfall throughout the year, with the lowest rainfall in the fall and winter from May to September. This is also when the lowest temperatures are encountered. Temperatures usually do not go below 30°F (-1°C) or above 82°F (28°C). The general conditions are relatively warm to cool and dry for most of the year.

Biology

The pancake is unique and is probably the most easily identified tortoise of all the tortoises. It is extremely flat in profile, which is the reason for its common name of pancake tortoise. Additionally, it is a rather small species, attaining a length of roughly 7 inches (18 cm). The shell color is normally dark brown, with a slightly lighter starburst pattern on each carapace scute. The plastron is normally a patternless light brown color.

Along with its flattened shape, the pancake tortoise has other unique attributes. The flat plastron remains relatively soft throughout the animal's life. This soft shell allows the tortoise to slip easily between the rocks in which it lives. When pancake tortoises do slip between the rocks, they do not inflate their lungs to wedge themselves between the rocks, as is commonly believed. What they do is rotate their arms to form a wedge. This locks them into the crevice and makes it difficult for a predator to get them out. Although the pancake tortoise seems to be at a disadvantage from the shape of its shell, it has very long legs and an agile neck. This allows the tortoise to easily

Pancake tortoises are adept climbers, and they are surprisingly fast and agile turtles.

right itself should it flip over.

The tortoise mainly restricts itself to the rock outcroppings, where its climbing skills are surpassed by no other tortoise. These skills can be described as nothing more than amazing. They use their wedging ability, long legs, and agile neck to enable them to traverse almost any surface.

There is no external distinguishing difference between the male and the female except for the length of tail. Males have much longer and thicker tails than the females. Females tend to stay slightly smaller, but this is not a reliable trait for sexing.

The pancake is believed to feed mostly on grasses and weeds that grow between the *kopjes* but is reported to feed on carrion as well. The tortoise quickly moves with the aid of its long legs and hyper manner from *kopje* to *kopje* as it feeds. Good numbers of pancakes may be found in a given *kopje*, and several will often shelter together in the same crevice.

The Pancake tortoise seems to prefer cooler temperatures in nature, and it will seek shelter when temperatures get too high. It has been found active at relatively cool temperatures in the range of 54° to 59°F (12 to 15°C). This seems to be the temperature at which it is comfortable and appears to be most active, but pancakes bask at these temperatures to raise their body temperatures considerably.

Breeding takes place during the warmer periods of the year, with mating being observed in January and February. This is the peak to end of the rainy season. The male and the female are extremely animated during breeding. The male will quickly chase and bite at the female, while at the same time trying to and flip her over in an effort to get her to remain still.

Nesting is believed to occur at the end of the dry season to the beginning of the rainy season, which indicates the tortoise probably carries the egg through the cooler period of the year. The female will produce only one large egg at each nesting but will nest several times through the season at roughly 30-day intervals. Nests are constructed in loose sandy soil. Incubation duration is between 170 and 230 days, with the hatchlings reported to emerge in December. Studies of this tortoise in the wild are incomplete when it comes to nesting and other aspects of its life. Further studies are required on the breeding behavior of this species in the wild.

Captive Care

Pancake tortoises are not often available, but they require mention because of their uniqueness and because some breeders have been successful in breeding this species. As we learn more about their husbandry, there is sure to be more frequent successful captive breeding. The most successful keepers of this species are those who provide an environment similar to the natural habitat.

Pancake tortoises are active tortoises that require plenty of space and a stimulating environment. Having an artificial *kopje* is paramount to getting this tortoise to thrive in captivity. The *kopje* can be as simple as setting up bricks with flat boards or slate stones between them to allow the tortoise to climb and feel secure while hidden between them. Keepers who want to get more elaborate can construct a mock *kopje* using wire mesh and concrete. Holes and crevices should be incorporated within it, allowing the tortoise to climb and retreat. The holes must be big enough for the adult size of the tortoise, unless the keeper intends to build a new one when the tortoise outgrows the original. There should be no concern about how high or steep the surfaces are, because pancake tortoises are more than able to climb rocky surfaces. They have been known to fall from great heights without injury. The climbing seems to be something they enjoy. The *kopje* must be stable; any rocks or bricks used in its construction cannot be able to shift or fall. Although pancakes are resilient to falling, they are not able to withstand heavy bricks falling on top of them.

Proper housing for pancakes includes rocky surfaces the tortoises can climb and crevices in which they can hide.

Feeding is similar to that of any other herbivorous tortoise. Offer grasses, dark leafy greens, and a pelleted diet. Water should be available at all times. Aside from needing climbing facilities, the care for this tortoise is not very different from other species in this chapter. Be very careful if housing these tortoises outdoors. They are accomplished escape artists, and their small size means they can easily be carried off by crows, hawks, and other birds. Having a screen top over the enclosure is recommended.

Breeding

Successful breeding in captivity was not accomplished until observations of the crucial role the pancake's rocky habitat plays in their behavior became available. Breeding in captivity occurs throughout the year with the same vigor that is observed in the wild. Eggs are deposited one at a time at approximately 30-day intervals, with the female nesting five or more times per year. Eggs incubated at a temperature of 80.5° to 86°F (27° to 30°C) hatch in 99 to 196 days. Occasionally eggs will incubate for as long as 340 days.

Recommendation

The unique attributes of the pancake tortoise make it one of the most desirable pet tortoises. However, it does require some specialized care and does not breed reliably. Pancakes are rare in the pet trade and threatened in nature. Until captive-bred pancakes become more available, they are best left in the hands of experienced keepers.

Red-Footed Tortoise (*Chelonoidis carbonaria*)

Origin

Red-footed tortoises are found in northern South America, from western Brazil and Bolivia up to Venezuela and down to Paraguay. They are also found on many of the Caribbean Islands and on some islands off Panama and Nicaragua. The range outside South America is thought to be the result of human introductions. This species is still often referred to by its former scientific name, *Geochelone carbonaria*.

The amount and brightness of the red coloration on red-footed tortoises varies greatly between individuals.

Habitat

Red-footed tortoises are mostly found at the edges of forests bordered by grasslands and low-lying shrubs. The areas it frequents usually are humid but not wet, and the entire range experiences wet and dry seasons. Many of these areas can be quite dry during the dry seasons. Yearly rainfall from Venezuela to the northernmost Caribbean islands on which the red-footed tortoise is found can range from 21 to 52 inches (53 to 132 cm), with average yearly temperatures of 67° to 90°F (19.5 to 32°C).

In the southernmost part of the range, it is found in thorn forests of the Gran Chaco, a semi-arid and hot lowland plain. The primary flora in this area is composed of grasses and thorny bushes. The Gran Chaco has a high yearly average of 52 inches (132 cm), but it is dry most of the year, and rainfall varies greatly across the region. The average temperatures are between 60° and 85°F (15.5° to 29.5°C).

Biology

The red-footed tortoise varies widely in appearance, depending on its region of origin. Many regional variations exist, although none have been formally recognized by being designated as subspecies. On the average the tortoise looks very similar to the yellow-footed tortoise (C. *denticulata*). Individuals are distinguished from the yellow-footed tortoise by the scales on the top of the head just behind the nasal openings. The yellow-footed has two distinct elongated scales side by side, and the red-footed has one enlarged scale or multiple scales in no particular pattern. The yellow-footed is larger on average than the red-footed.

The length of adult red-footed tortoises ranges from 10 inches to over 24 inches (25.5 to 61 cm), with the largest coming from Colombia and the smallest coming from Paraguay and various island populations. The carapace is elongated and domed, with the color being dark brown fading to yellow in spots where the primary shell has been worn away. Some populations have a mottled or radiated pattern on both the upper shell and the plastron. The head and scale color can be from bright red to orange to dull yellow.

Redfoots inhabit grasslands and the forests bordering them. They are not often found deep within true rain forests.

The males tend to be somewhat peanut-shaped, having a narrow waist between the front and hind legs. The males have deeply concave plastrons and long pointy tails. The females are consistently oval in shape, with short stubby tails and flat plastrons. In the northern portion of its range the red-footed tortoise's activities accord to the wet and dry seasons. The tortoises are most active during the wet and rainy seasons. They will bed down and become inactive during the dry

Redfoots are hardy and adaptable tortoises.

seasons but will emerge if the unusual rainstorm should present itself. Where the tortoise occurs in the Gran Chaco it will estivate during the hot periods and hibernate during cold periods. It will seek refuge in animal burrows during cold periods, and it is not uncommon to find more than one tortoise sharing the same refuge.

When the tortoise is active it is an omnivorous and opportunistic feeder. It feeds on greens along with fruit and carrion. It has also been known to take insects (and their larvae) as well as worms, but it is more inclined to eat plant matter. This species has been known to cover long distances when foraging for food or searching for a mate. The red-footed tortoise is an avid swimmer and is neither afraid of nor incapable of crossing deep water should the need arise.

Breeding takes place during the rainy season throughout most of its natural range. Tortoises will become active with the onset of consistent rains. The males will seek out females and will engage in territorial displays with other males when they are encountered. These encounters almost seem to have a social function, and the tortoises will bob their heads in a very specific fashion. If one or the other male does not respond accordingly, a battle ensues until one or the other gives up. The battle usually consists of nothing more than ramming face to face in a type of "push of war." When the male finds a suitable female he will pursue the female while bobbing his head. If the female is receptive or the male manages to corner her, he climbs onto her back. During copulation the male emits clucking and honking sounds as he bobs his head and opens his mouth. He is very loud can be heard from amazing distances. The female will nest after a successful mating. She will deposit 2 to 15 eggs in a well-formed flask-shaped nest. She can nest several times in a season. It can take three to six months for the hatchlings to emerge, depending on the population of red-footed tortoise as well as the incubation conditions.

Captive Care

The red-footed tortoise is one of the most popular tortoises kept in captivity. It has been successfully bred on tortoise farms within its home range and by private individuals inside and

Red vs. Yellow

The red-footed tortoise occupies habitat that is drier than that preferred by the yellow-footed tortoise, but there is some overlap. Where this overlap occurs, the red-footed usually is more plentiful.

There is some speculation that the elaborate head movements the two species display during courtship and territorial conflicts is one mechanism that prevents the nterbreeding of the red-footed and yellow-footed tortoises. It is thought that females of one species do not respond to the head-bobbing patterns of the other species, only to that of their own.

outside of the natural range for many years. Wild-caught adults are unfortunately still being imported, and these animals require the same special care needed by wild-caught specimens of other species: they need to be rehydrated, treated for parasites, and monitored closely. The adults do not acclimate well and require a great deal of work to establish—and still the odds of success are poor. In contrast, capive-bred redfoots are hardy pets.

There are several localized forms of the red-footed tortoise that vary from each other in color, adult size, and body shape. However, it is impossible to know where most of the ones in the pet trade originated, because collection data is often nonexistent. Additionally, breeders surely have paired tortoises from different populations together. This is true with one exception: the cherry-head red-footed tortoise. This is a smaller form of red-footed tortoise that usually reaches only 10 to 12 inches (25.5 to 30.5 cm) SCL. This variety has a mottled pattern on the carapace and plastron. The red scales on the head often are especially vibrant, which is why they are called cherry-heads. They are very cold tolerant, while the other red-footed tortoises are susceptible to

respiratory problems if temperatures are too cool. The cherry-heads seem to be hardier tortoises. The exact range of the cherry-head variety is not known but is believed to be in southern Brazil.

Captive care for C. *carbonaria* is straightforward, with some minor notations. It is important to maintain this species at an acceptable temperature; that can be difficult in cooler climates, because the tortoise can get too large for indoor maintenance by the average keeper. This species should be kept in a temperature range of 80° to 90°F (26.5° to 32°C).

The red-footed tortoise should have access to water at all times. Although a pool is not necessary, one would be used if provided. The tortoise does not need a moist environment, although a humid hide is extremely beneficial. A moist section in the enclosure is more than the tortoise needs to thrive. Many keepers believe that the red-footed tortoise needs it moist, and this usually leads to shell problems, such as shell rot. In actuality, redfoots come from relatively dry environments with seasonal high humidity.

The cherry-head redfoot is popular with keepers and breeders because of its brighter colors and (usually) smaller size compared to the more common redfoot.

These tortoises do well on the usual dark leafy greens and vegetables along with occasional fruit. They do exceptionally well on a pellet diet when it is added to a diet based on greens and fruit. Animal protein is not required, but they do consume it in nature; a small amount should cause no harm.

Breeding

Breeding takes place during the spring and summer; eggs are deposited throughout the summer, fall, and early winter. Red-footed tortoises that breed in captivity follow the same behavior patterns described above. The female can lay 2 to 15 eggs, which should hatch in 116 to 118 days if incubated at a temperature of 77° to 86°F (25° to 30°C).

Recommendation

The red-footed tortoise is one the easiest tortoises to obtain, especially as captive-bred individuals. The recommended form is the cherry-head red-footed tortoise because of its hardiness and the fact that it stays relatively small. All red-footed tortoises are equally personable and enjoyable to keep. This species, especially the cherry-headed variety, is highly recommended to tortoise keepers.

Chelonoidis denticulata

Chapter 8

Tropical Forest Species

The tropical forest species are the most specialized group of tortoises available to hobbyists. While they can tolerate relatively dry conditions for some time, they fare best and seem most at ease when the climate is warm and wet. It is for this reason a humid environment is needed for the species covered here. The forest species include the popular yellow-footed tortoise, the enormous Asian brown tortoise, and the odd forest hinge-backed tortoise.

Asian Brown Tortoise (*Manouria emys*)

Origin

This species is found across southern Asia from Assam in eastern India to Malaysia and some Indonesian islands, including Sumatra and Borneo. It is also called the Asian forest tortoise, the Burmese brown tortoise, and the Burmese mountain tortoise.

Habitat

The Asian Brown Tortoise is a true tropical rain forest tortoise; it inhabits densely forested areas of evergreens up to 3,300 feet (1,006 m) in altitude. The tortoise's preferred habitat is wet forests near rivers and streams. It seems to enjoy burrowing into moist soil and rotting leaf litter. Asian browns sometimes forage within bodies of water. Rainfall within much of the natural habitat may be greater than 60 inches (152.5 cm), with much of that falling between April and October.

Other Forest Species

The entries in this chapter give a common sampling of the available forest species. There are other tortoises from similar habitats that can be kept like these. One such species is the elongated tortoise (*Indotestudo elongata*), found from India to Borneo; another is the closely related Tranvacore tortoise (*Indotestudo travancoria*) of southwestern India. The flat-tailed tortoise (*Pyxis planicauda*) is a small, endangered turtle from Madagascar that should be kept like a forest species.

Elongated tortoise

The Asian brown tortoise dwells mostly in wet, often mountainous, forests across Southeast Asia.

Biology

The Asian brown tortoise is the largest Asian tortoise and the fourth largest of all tortoises. It can attain a length of up to 23.5 inches (60 cm) and weigh over 88 pounds (40 kg). There are large tubercles on the back of each leg. The male's plastron is usually concave, but this is not always the case. The tail of the male tortoise is usually longer and thicker than that of the female tortoise. The tail of the male sometimes has a horny scale at the tip.

Two subspecies are recognized, and they show some significant differences. *Manouria emys emys* occurs the southern portion of the range, in southern Thailand, Malaysia, Borneo, and Sumatra. It is a large olive brown to dark brown tortoise usually with no special markings to distinguish it from any other tortoise. Occasionally they will display a faint dark brown radiated pattern. The shell shape is oval and not very high domed which gives the tortoise a relatively flat appearance. The pectoral scutes of the plastron (the scutes right behind the front legs) do not meet in the middle—they are widely separated. This is the most reliable way to distinguish this subspecies from the other one, *M. emys phayrei*. In *M. emys phayrei* these scutes meet at the midline. *Manouria emys phayrei* occupies the northern part of the range in Assam, Burma, and northern Thailand. The carapace of this subspecies is often more domed than that of *M. emys emys*. Although *M. emys phayrei* is sometimes called the Burmese black tortoise, it is not always black, and you cannot tell the two apart based on coloration. *M. emys emys* tends to stay much smaller than *M. emys phayrei*.

The diet of *Manouria* consists mostly of broadleaf weeds, in addition to water plants and tubers foraged from streams. Bamboo shoots are also consumed. The tortoise is thought to be an opportunistic feeder, consuming fungi, roots, insects, and carrion in addition to various leaves and fruit.

Asian brown tortoises are most active in the early morning and late afternoon hours, and it is at these times that most feeding and breeding occurs. Breeding is similar to the mating of other tortoises except that the male is extremely animated and vocal emitting various sounds while bobbing his head up and down and side to side. If breeding is successful the female will deposit 23 to 51 eggs within the months of April and May or September and October. The eggs are spherical and 51 to 54 mm in diameter. The eggs normally hatch in 63 to 69 days, and the hatchlings emerge a size of 2.3 to 2.6 inches (60 to 66 mm) SCL.

Manouria are unique tortoises when it comes to nesting. The female actually constructs a complex nest by first scraping leaf litter, soil, and detritus in a pile before she actually nests. She hen deposits the eggs within the mound, where she will sit on the nest and appear to guard the nest for several days. The leaf mound not only protects the eggs, but it also provides heat created during the decomposition of the mound.

Captive Care

Asian brown tortoises are one of the more complex tortoises to keep because they get quite large and have fairly exacting requirements. Providing the correct humidity and temperature is key to having a brown tortoise thrive. This would be extremely difficult to accomplish in an indoor environment. A minimum enclosure size for a pair of these turtles would be 10 feet square and a larger one would be even better. If kept outdoors, a well-planted enclosure is a

Successful captive-breeding of the Asian brown tortoise is not common, and few breeders produce this species consistently.

Another *Manouria*

A third form of *Manouria* exists, and it is considered a separate species, *M. impressa*, the impressed tortoise. It seems to occur in Burma, Malaysia, Thailand, Laos, Vietnam, Cambodia, and southern China, but the species has not been thoroughly studied in the wild. The impressed tortoise lives in dry forests, often high in the mountains. It tends to do very poorly in captivity.

must. They enjoy having plenty of shade and cover. A mulch substrate of roughly 2 feet (61 cm) deep is the best substrate to help maintain humidity and allow the tortoises to dig.

A good temperature range for this species is 75° to 85°F (24° to 29.5°C), and they do not appear to be fond of basking at higher temperatures. Provide a heated shelter when temperatures drop below 75°F (24°C), although Asian browns are rather cold tolerant. A water container such as a cement pool or cement mixing tray should be sunk into the substrate to allow soaking. This tortoise seems to enjoy rain showers and mistings. A relative humidity of about 80 percent (with some variation) is suggested, but give the tortoise an area where it can dry off if it desires.

Feed Asian browns a mostly herbivorous diet supplemented with a good formulated tortoise diet and calcium carbonate. A small amount of fruit and fungi can be added to the diet as a treat. Grasses and broadleafed plants are readily consumed and should be the mainstay of the diet.

Breeding

Breeding is not very common for this tortoise, but those keepers who setup their tortoises properly have been successful—although not usually consistent—at breeding this species. Clutch size and incubation duration are as given in the previous section. It appears that the only method to get this species to breed is to provide a naturalistic habitat.

Recommendations

The Asian Brown tortoise has been a challenge for many keepers. There are a relatively good number of hobbyists who have been successful raising and breeding these great tortoises. The babies are easy to maintain, but they do not stay small. This is a tortoise that is recommended for people who live in a warm humid climate or for the rare keeper who can provide suitable indoor accommodations. Wild-caught Asian brown tortoises make their way into the pet trade but should be left to the zoos and highly experienced tortoise keepers because they often fail to acclimate. Wild-caught Asian browns have become less common because they are protected in portions of their natural range.

Forest Hinge-Backed tortoise (*Kinixys erosa*)

Origin

This species occurs along coastal West Africa from Gambia to Gabon and inland to Rwanda and Uganda. Other common

The hinge-backed tortoises are named for the unique hinge-like structure in the carapace (circled), allowing it to move down and cover the hind end. This is the forest hingeback.

names for *Kinixys erosa* include the serrated hinge-backed tortoise and Schweigger's tortoise. Home's hingeback (*K. homeana*) is sometimes also called the forest hingeback, leading to confusion between the two species.

In nature, forest hingebacks live in swamps and wet forests. They need warm, humid, and low-lit conditions in captivity.

Habitat

The primary habitat is lowland forest, which covers most of the forest hingeback's range. The habitat is poorly drained and consists mostly of rivers and swamps with hardwood trees and lush undergrowth. The climate is normally hot and humid, with dry and wet seasons. The wet season runs from April to October, the rest of the year being the dry season. The wet season is also the cooler season, but the temperature within the habitat rarely falls below 60°F (15.5°C) or rises above 100°F (38°C) at any point in the year.

Biology

The forest hingeback is one of the larger hinge-backed tortoises but is considered a medium-size tortoise, measuring approximately 12 inches (30.5 cm) SCL as an adult. The males are larger than the females of the same age. It is identified by its hinged aft carapace similar to that of Bell's hinge-backed tortoise, but the marginal scutes present a scalloped appearance. The tortoise is normally dark brown with white accent markings on each scute. The carapace is rounded and slopes gently to the tail—in the similar Home's hingeback, the top of the carapace has a sharp drop to the rear. Males have longer gular scutes in addition to a longer tail and a concave plastron when compared to females.

Forest hingebacks prefer the moistest of the habitats in their range. The species is extremely comfortable in an aquatic environment and is an avid swimmer. Forest hingebacks are often found resting in water. When they are on land they spend most of their time foraging under leaf litter and debris or buried under logs and branches. The tortoise is active mostly at night, when it forages for food and looks for a mate. It is reported to have a very large home range

The diet of forest hingebacks should include more animal matter than the diet of most other tortoises.

and will travel long distances over land and through water. The tortoise will spend equally long periods buried down under whatever cover it can find.

The feeding habits of the forest hingeback are similar to those of the other hinge-backed tortoises. It is omnivorous in nature, feeding mainly on leaves and fruit. It appears to be especially fond of mushrooms and other fungi, along with earthworms. The tortoise also eats insects, snails, and slugs. Forest hingebacks feed opportunistically on carrion, for which they are well adapted with sharp beaks and strong jaws.

Breeding takes place throughout the year and through all hours of the day and night. Male-to-male combat has been rarely observed, but the mating process between the male and the female is quite active. The male will ram and run around the female, occasionally flipping her over. During the mating process the male will emit a series of loud hisses and squeaks during copulation. The female tortoise will deposit one to five eggs in a clutch and will nest several times in a season. The tortoise does not dig a proper nest as most tortoises do but deposits the eggs on the ground and covers then with leaf litter or detritus; the eggs can remain from 110 to 300 days, depending on how much sun exposure they get. Due to the heavy overgrowth of the habitat sunshine is not constant.

Captive Care

Imported adults are always difficult to acclimate because of their specialized needs and the behavioral imprint the tortoises bring from their life in the wild. These tortoises come from a hot and moist environment and often suffer from severe dehydration during capture and transport. They also have the added burden of internal and external parasites, which flourish in the climate the tortoises come from. Any imported forest hinge-backed tortoise should be treated for worms and protozoans as a precaution; nearly all imported specimens will have a heavy parasite load. Additionally, these turtles can be problematic feeders. Try a wide variety of foods and don't rule out any choices. Your goal is to get the tortoise to eat something—you can switch it to a healthy diet later. Keepers report that earthworms, melons, and mushrooms are often successful at tempting a forest hingeback to eat.

The tortoise should be set up in a moist environment but needs areas where it can dry off. This is the opposite of providing a humid hide in that you are providing a dry place within the moist environment. If humidity is too low, this species often develops inflamed eyes and starts wheezing. A pool should be provided so the tortoise can not only soak but actually swim, since this is so important to its natural behavior. Obviously, you must make sure the turtle can easily exit the water to avoid drowning. Hydration is critical for this species; weekly (or even more frequent) soaking of forest hingebacks is highly recommended.

Forest hingebacks are shy turtles, and they become stressed easily. It is recommended that the enclosure be well planted and/or that many hiding places be provided. Hiding places should be humid, but at least on hide should be dry to give the tortoise a chance to dry off a bit. Forest hingebacks are agile climbers, so the enclosure should be especially secure to eliminate the possibility of escape. Making the tortoise feel at home will reduce the desire for the tortoise to escape or wander. Temperatures should be in the range of 75° to 85°F (24° to 29.5°C). Forest hingbacks do not seem to like bright light. A fluorescent lamp is recommended over incandescent lights because of the lower light levels it will provide.

The best chance to get these tortoises to feed is to offer foods that they would encounter in the wild: mushrooms, fruit, earthworms, and small fish. If the tortoise can be encouraged to take pellets, half the feeding battle is won. This can be accomplished by scenting the pellets with any foods that the tortoise is accepting. Diet should be as varied as possible, with probably about 20 percent of the diet being animal products. Most of the animal matter in the diet should consist

Home's Hinge-Backed Tortoise

Home's hinge-backed tortoise (*K. homeana*) is another hingeback found in the wet equatorial forests of Africa, from the Ivory Coast and Nigeria to the Democratic Republic of Congo. It is similar in habitat, diet, behavior, and appearance to *Kinixys erosa*. There is some confusion between the two, and both have been imported under the label "forest hingeback." The best way to tell the two species apart is to look at the angle between the top of the carapace and posterior of the carapace. In the forest hingeback there is a slope down from the top to the back. In Home's hingeback the top and the back are almost perpendicular and meet at a nearly right angle. This difference is more pronounced in adults than in juveniles. Home's hingeback is somewhat smaller than the forest hingeback. The two species can be kept in the same conditions and fed the same diet.

of earthworms and feeder insects, such as mealworms, wax worms, and silkworms (they can have trouble catching more mobile feeder insects, such as crickets). Although this is not recommended for most other tortoises, keepers can safely feed this species pinky mice, snails, whole feeder fish, and water-packed no-salt canned salmon or shrimp on occasion. These tortoises generally are not fond of greens, so you may need to mix them well with the foods your turtle likes better.

Breeding

Breeding of *Kinixys erosa* is extremely rare, and information on the subject is sparse. That should not discourage any keeper from working with this tortoise, because working with rarely bred species is how new and more successful methods are uncovered. Eggs have successfully hatched when incubated at 86° to 88°F (30° to 31°C) and 90 percent humidity. It can take 120 to 400 days for the eggs to hatch.

Recommendation

The forest hingeback is not normally recommended for the beginning tortoise keeper, because of its specialized needs and the fact that most available individuals are wild-caught. This tortoise is rarely bred in captivity, but individuals are commonly kept by hobbyists. Even though the forest hingeback is not recommended for the beginning tortoise keeper, some beginners have been among the most successful keepers and breeders of this species. The forest hinge-backed tortoise is a fascinating and worthwhile challenge if the keeper does the proper research before obtaining one. This is an exceptionally bad impulse-buy tortoise.

Yellow-Footed Tortoise (*Chelonoidis denticulata*)

Origin

This species inhabits the Amazonian lowlands of Venezuela south to Bolivia and Ecuador and east to northeastern Brazil. There are introduced populations on the islands of Trinidad, Tobago, and Guadeloupe. This species is commonly referred to by its former scientific name *Geochelone denticulata*.

Habitat

The yellow-footed tortoise is restricted to undisturbed areas of the tropical rainforests of the Amazon River basin, although it has been

Originally native to the Amazon Basin, the yellow-footed tortoise has been introduced to several Caribbean islands.

in introduced into other habitats. The area it inhabits is typified by thick forest canopy consisting of tropical evergreen and deciduous trees along with heavy underbrush. The average temperature is 79°F (26°C), with an average rainfall of 80 inches (203 cm) per year. These conditions

Adult yellowfoots are large tortoises—the one pictured is 36 inches (91.5 cm) long—that require spacious enclosures.

provide for a constantly high humidity. The forest floor has a consistently thick covering of detritus and leaf litter along with rotting logs and branches.

Biology

The yellowfoot is an elongated tortoise that is dark brown in color except where the dark color has been worn away to reveal a light yellow color—that is true on both the carapace and the plastron. The wearing away usually occurs at the center of the individual carapace scutes. The wear may be fairly extensive, giving it the appearance of being yellow with dark brown accents along the growth lines of the scutes. The head and scales are usually a light yellow color with very little variation. To distinguish the yellow-footed tortoise from the red-footed tortoise, refer to the section on the latter species.

On the average, adult yellow-footed tortoises range from 12 to 15 inches (30 to 40 cm) SCL. Certain populations—seemingly restricted to the lower Amazon River basin—can attain lengths over 35 inches (90 cm).

The male of the species is peanut-shaped, with a deeply concave plastron and a very elongated tail. The male's anal scutes are wide and fairly parallel to the lateral axis of the tortoise. The female yellow-footed tortoise is the same in color but is more oval in shape, with a flat plastron and a relatively short tail. The anal scutes of the female form a U in shape.

The yellow-footed tortoise is a secretive species that spends most of its time foraging through dense underbrush. It is most active early in the morning and late afternoon. It is an omnivorous turtle that will feed on anything that catches its attention, including insects and carrion. This species has been observed congregating under fruiting trees to gorge itself on the fallen ripe fruit. They are reported to be a major seed dispersal mechanism for these trees.

Throughout this tortoise's historic range there is a minor seasonal change between wet and dry season that does influence its behavioral activity. Breeding does not seem to be seasonal but that varies by the specific population and local conditions. The common pattern is that all seem to breed during the onset of rain or exceptionally high humidity.

One interesting observation is that when a male mates with a certain female in a season, he will continue to seek out that particular female for breeding throughout the season. The yellow-footed tortoise has a mating ritual similar to that of the red-footed tortoise but different enough so that when two males of the different species encounter each other combat does not occur. When two male yellowfoots encounter each other, one will initiate a sequence of head movements. If this is responded to in kind by the encountered tortoise a battle usually ensues. A female will not respond in kind, which seems to be a signal that the male can mate with her. The male yellow-footed tortoise is vocal as it mounts to mate the female and during mating. A mating male will emit a honking noise from its outstretched head and open mouth.

Nesting is usually triggered during the onset of a dry period. The eggs are deposited anywhere from bare ground to a deep, well-constructed nest. At times the eggs are deposited in a depression or bare ground covered with leaf litter. The eggs are then lightly covered over by the leaf litter and left in place. A female yellow-footed tortoise will normally deposit three to ten eggs that hatch in 95 to 180 days.

Captive Care

The yellow-footed tortoise does not tolerate dry environments, but it has always been a favorite of hobbyists living in humid environments. These tortoises are being imported, so keepers need to be aware that wild-caught yellow-footed tortoises are extremely difficult to acclimate to captivity. The wild-caught tortoises are shy and

An enclosure housing yellowfoots should include a pool because this species seems to enjoy soaking and swimming.

usually infested with internal and external parasites. They are also imprinted with a specific feeding pattern, which can make them refuse to eat offered food. The yellow-footed tortoise is being raised on tortoise farms with good success, and some breeders have had some success with this species, making it easy to obtain a captive-born and -raised individual.

These tortoises can get very large, so it is important to have either good indoor facilities or a well-planted outdoor enclosure in a climatic zone that allows the tortoise to remain outdoors all year. Yellowfoots need tropical temperatures in the range of 80° to 95°F (25.5° to 35°C). The presence of high humidity is extremely important with this species. Yellowfoots seem to prefer a dimly lit enclosure; outdoor enclosures for this species should be well-planted with plenty of hiding places. The enclosure should have a pool that lets tortoise easily enter and exit, because the yellow-footed tortoise loves the water. It will spend a great amount of time swimming and soaking in the pool.

Feeding captive-bred yellow-footed tortoises is not problematic. They should be offered fibrous vegetables combined with dark leafy greens and some fruit. The occasional feeding of a pellet diet is also beneficial to this tortoise. Yellowfoots do not require animal matter in the diet, but offering some occasionally will do no harm.

Breeding

The yellow-footed tortoise usually is captive-bred only within a climate that is similar to its natural one; success outside of the tropics and subtropics is rare. The most successful keepers

Most successful yellowfoot breeders live in tropical or subtropical climates and house the tortoises outdoors.

of this species are those who live in warm humid areas where the tortoises can be left undisturbed as much as possible. Breeding will occur during the warmer parts of the year, and females may produce two or three clutches annually. In captivity, they produce up to a dozen eggs that hatch out in 120 to 180 days at temperatures of 77° to 86°F (25° to 30°C). However, hatching can take as long as 270 days.

Recommendation

The yellow-footed tortoise can be difficult to raise and acclimate but is well worth the effort. It grows to become a large and impressive tortoise with an outgoing personality once it has become established and accustomed to its surroundings. Yellowfoots are probably not the best species for beginners, but a conscientious first-time keeper who obtains a well-started captive-bred tortoise has a good chance of success.

It is hoped that this guide has not only provided some direction but also some inspiration to the new tortoise keeper. It is also hoped that it has provided some new hints or new ideas for the more experienced keeper. A single book cannot provide all the information a keeper is looking for without being a monster of a tome. This guide is intended to be a reliable guide but not a source of all the information you might want or need. It is a source of information that a keeper can quickly refer to as needed. It was written to suggest to new keepers some good ideas on how to maintain their tortoises in captivity while also providing a small look into the natural history of some of the tortoises available.

It should be understood that the format of the guide allows for some crossover information, meaning that the same suggestions for care may apply to several different species. While not all available species were given their own accounts, each of the species chapters discusses the tortoises that have similar care requirements that those that do have their own accounts.

There is one point that cannot be stressed enough and that is every tortoise keeper is going to have different convictions and different husbandry styles. There is no such thing as a best way to keep a tortoise. There is such a thing as providing the husbandry that allows a tortoise to be healthy and thriving. The exact methods to do so will differ from keeper to keeper and tortoise to tortoise. The goal of every keeper is to provide the best care for his or her tortoise. By keeping this goal in mind and researching the needs of the species you keep, you are well on your way to having a healthy and long-lived tortoise.

Resources
Conservation Groups
The Tortoise Trust
BM Tortoise
London
WC1N 3XX
UK
www.tortoisetrust.org/

World Chelonian Trust
P.O. Box 1445
Vacaville, CA 95696
www.chelonia.org/

Rescue and Adoption Servies
American Tortoise Rescue
23852 Pacific Coast Highway, Suite 928
Malibu, CA 90265
Phone: 800-938-3553
Email: info@tortoise.com
http://www.tortoise.com/

Mid-Atlantic Turtle & Tortoise Society
P.O. Box 23686
Baltimore, MD 21203
E-mail: matts@matts-turtles.org
www.matts-turtles.org/

New England Amphibian and Reptile Rescue
www.ReptileRescue.ne

Veterinary Resources
Association of Reptile and Amphibian Veterinarians (ARAV)
P.O. Box 605
Chester Heights, PA 19017
Phone: 610-358-9530
E-mail: ARAVETS@aol.com
www.arav.org

Websites
Chelonian Research Foundation
www.chelonian.org

Leopardtortoise.com
www.leopardtortoise.com

Melissa Kaplan's Herp Care Collection
www.anapsid.org

The Russian Tortoise
www.russiantortoise.org

The Sulcata and Leopard Tortoise
www.africantortoise.com

Tortoisecare.org
www.tortoisecare.org

About the Author:

E.J. Pirog has been keeping a large group of reptiles with a special focus on tortoises for more than 30 years. He frequently writes and lectures on turtle-related topics and is the author of two previous books on tortoises. He lives near Atlanta, Georgia, with his family and a herd of tortoises.

Photo Credits:

Florian Andronache (from Shutterstock): 36, 149
Ayazad (from Shutterstock): 114
Pierre-Yves Babelon (from Shutterstock): 1
R. D. Bartlett: 10, 32, 117, 165, 173
Boris15 (from Shutterstock): 152
EcoPrint (from Shutterstock): 158
Christopher Elwell (from Shutterstock): 69
Zadiraka Evgenii (from Shutterstock): 74
Fivespots (from Shutterstock): 15, 101, 136, 161, 169, 174, 176, and back cover
Isabelle Francais: 30, 58
Paul Freed: 97, 147
Karel Gallas (from Shutterstock); 138
Darrin Henry (from Shutterstock): 140
Elpis Ioannidis (from Shutterstock): 91
Eric Isselée (from Shutterstock): 4,
Iusubov (from Shutterstock): 48
Jagodka (from Shutterstock): 123
S.G. James (from Shutterstock): 144
Natalie Jean (from Shutterstock): 184
Johafil (from Shutterstock): 38
Mariusz S. Jurgielewicz (from Shutterstock): 22

Jerry R. Loll: 129
Daniel Loretto (from Shutterstock): 102
Sean McKeown: 85, 89, 153, 177, 178
Susan C.Miller: 154
J.J. Morales (from Shutterstock): 135
Richard Peterson (from Shutterstock): 19 (bottom)
M. P. and C. Piednoir: 81, 166
Jonathan Plant: 150
Kristina Postnikova (from Shutterstock): 130
Annabel Ross: 111
P. A. Rutledge: 26
John R. Smith (from Shutterstock): 54
Mark Smith: 13
Alexey Stiop (from Shutterstock): 6, 181
Karl H. Switak: 20, 100, 126, 146, 151, 156, 162, 167, 170
Vinicius Tupinamba (from Shutterstock): front cover
Jacqueline Watson (from Shutterstock): 8
Tom Willard (from Shutterstock): 124, 134
Pan Xunbin (from Shutterstock): 172

All other photos by the author

Species Illustrated by Page:

Aldabra tortoise: 8, 39, 52, 71, 140, 143, 144
Asian brown tortoise: 117, 173, 174
Bell's hinge-backed tortoise: 122, 145, 146, 147
bowsprit tortoise: 85
desert tortoise: 137
Egyptian tortoise: 87, 126
elongated tortoise: 172
flat-tailed tortoise: 79
forest hinge-backed tortoise: 15, 176, 177, 178, and back cover
gopher tortoise: 112
Greek tortoise: 30, 34, 36, 48, 67, 110, 121, 127, 128, 129, 149, 150, 151, 152
Hermann's tortoise: 10, 19, 58, 102, 153, 154, 155, 156

Home's hinge-backed tortoise: 32
impressed tortoise: 104, 175
leopard tortoise: 27, 38, 44, 56, 82, 96, 99, 100, 106, 118, 119, 138, 157, 158, 159, 160
marginated tortoise: 66, 81, 91
pancake tortoise: 97, 161, 162, 164
radiated tortoise: 1, 89
red-footed tortoise: 42, 49, 73, 165, 166, 167, 169, and front cover
Russian tortoise: 19, 20, 24, 29, 74, 83, 114, 130, 132, 133
Speke's hinge-backed tortoise: 62
spider tortoise: 35, 43, 141
star tortoise: 13, 76
sulcata tortoise: 12, 17, 22, 26, 60, 69, 71, 101, 124, 134, 135, 136
yellow-footed tortoise: 6, 170, 181, 182, 183, 184

Index

Boldfaced numbers indicate illustrations.

WHERE REPTILES RULE

For the beginner and experienced
reptile keeper, Zilla products help
to maintain your animals' health, activity and longevity.

From complete tropical or desert kits to the foods and
accessories for their everyday needs, we have a wide
range of quality products for the care of your reptile.

The Zilla brand is where reptiles rule!

Zilla®
zilla-rules.com - 888.255.4527